Heaven, Hell, *and* HOPE

Heaven, Hell, *and* HOPE

A Biblical and Theological Exploration of Universal Salvation

Chris Kugler

Published by Baker Academic
a division of Baker Publishing Group
Grand Rapids, Michigan
BakerAcademic.com

Printed in the United States of America

Library of Congress Cataloging-in-Publication Data
Names: Kugler, Chris, author.
Title: Heaven, hell, and hope : a biblical and theological exploration of universal salvation / Chris Kugler.
Description: Grand Rapids, Michigan : Baker Academic, a division of Baker Publishing Group, [2025] | Includes bibliographical references and indexes.
Identifiers: LCCN 2025003645 | ISBN 9781540965158 (paperback) | ISBN 9781540968340 (casebound) | ISBN 9781493447633 (ebook) | ISBN 9781493447640 (pdf)
Subjects: LCSH: Universalism. | Hell—Christianity. | Heaven—Christianity. | Hope—Religious aspects—Christianity. | Salvation—Biblical teaching. | Eschatology, Jewish.
Classification: LCC BX9941.3 .K845 2025 | DDC 289.1/34—dc23/eng/20250326
LC record available at https://lccn.loc.gov/2025003645

Unless otherwise indicated, quotations of Scripture and other ancient sources are the author's own translation.

Cover design by Paula Gibson

Baker Publishing Group publications use paper produced from sustainable forestry practices and postconsumer waste whenever possible.

25 26 27 28 29 30 31 7 6 5 4 3 2 1

For Jack and Tom, sure-footed guides

And for Litty, Blaze, and Pickle, all my reasons

Contents

Acknowledgments

Heartfelt thanks go to

Dave Nelson, for believing in the project;

Bryan Dyer, for clear vision, shrewd advice, and consistent encouragement;

Dustyn Keepers, for numerous helpful suggestions;

Alex DeMarco and Brandon Benziger, for making this a much better book than it would have been;

Markus Bockmuehl, for such generous hospitality at Keble College, Oxford.

"Dowl," for not letting me think about anything else;

Larry and Gail, my parents, for always believing in me;

Hank, my little buddy;

Eli and Brady, my perfect "bitty pwoblems";

And Katie Rae, my beauty and joy, for support "pressed down, shaken together, and running over."

Abbreviations

Old Testament

Gen.	Genesis	Prov.	Proverbs
Exod.	Exodus	Isa.	Isaiah
Deut.	Deuteronomy	Jer.	Jeremiah
Judg.	Judges	Dan.	Daniel
1 Sam.	1 Samuel	Mal.	Malachi

New Testament

Matt.	Matthew	1 Thess.	1 Thessalonians
Rom.	Romans	2 Thess.	2 Thessalonians
1 Cor.	1 Corinthians	1 Tim.	1 Timothy
2 Cor.	2 Corinthians	Heb.	Hebrews
Gal.	Galatians	1 Pet.	1 Peter
Eph.	Ephesians	2 Pet.	2 Peter
Phil.	Philippians	Rev.	Revelation
Col.	Colossians		

Old Testament Apocrypha / Deuterocanonical Books

1–2 Esd.	1–2 Esdras	Tob.	Tobit
Jdt.	Judith	Wis.	Wisdom (of Solomon)
1–4 Macc.	1–4 Maccabees		

Other Ancient Writings

Apoc. Paul	Apocalypse of Paul
Apoc. Pet.	Apocalypse of Peter
Apoc. Sedr.	Apocalypse of Sedrach
Apoc. Zeph.	Apocalypse of Zephaniah
Ascen. Isa.	Martyrdom and Ascension of Isaiah 6–11
b. Sanh.	Babylonian tractate Sanhedrin
2 Bar.	2 Baruch
3 Bar.	3 Baruch
Eccl. Rab.	Ecclesiastes Rabbah
1 En.	1 Enoch
2 En.	2 Enoch
Gen. Rab.	Genesis Rabbah
Gr. Apoc. Ezra	Greek Apocalypse of Ezra
Josephus, *Ant.*	Josephus, *Jewish Antiquities*
Josephus, *J.W.*	Josephus, *Jewish War*
LAE	Life of Adam and Eve
m. ʾAbot	Mishnaic tractate ʾAbot
Philo, *Moses*	Philo, *On the Life of Moses*
Philo, *QG*	Philo, *Questions and Answers on Genesis*
Pirqe R. El.	Pirqe Rabbi Eliezer
Ques. Ezra	Questions of Ezra
Sib. Or.	Sibylline Oracles
T. Ab.	Testament of Abraham
T. Mos.	Testament of Moses

Bibliographic

AB	Anchor Bible
ABD	*Anchor Bible Dictionary*. Edited by David Noel Freedman. 6 vols. New York: Doubleday, 1992
BBR	*Bulletin for Biblical Research*
BECNT	Baker Exegetical Commentary on the New Testament
BMSEC	Baylor–Mohr Siebeck Studies in Early Christianity
BNTC	Black's New Testament Commentary
BZAW	Beihefte zur Zeitschrift für die alttestamentliche Wissenschaft
BZNW	Beihefte zur Zeitschrift für die neutestamentliche Wissenschaft
CBQ	*Catholic Biblical Quarterly*
CBR	*Currents in Biblical Research*
CSBPHP	Cambridge Source Books in Post-Hellenistic Philosophy

DOTP	*Dictionary of the Old Testament Prophets*. Edited by Mark J. Boda and J. Gordon McConville. Downers Grove, IL: IVP Academic, 2012
DPL	*Dictionary of Paul and His Letters: A Compendium of Contemporary Biblical Scholarship*. Edited by Scot McKnight. 2nd ed. Downers Grove, IL: IVP Academic, 2023
HeyJ	*Heythrop Journal*
HTS	Harvard Theological Studies
ICC	International Critical Commentary
JSNT	*Journal for the Study of the New Testament*
LCL	Loeb Classical Library
LNTS	Library of New Testament Studies
NICNT	New International Commentary on the New Testament
NIGTC	New International Greek Testament Commentary
NovT	*Novum Testamentum*
NovTSup	Supplements to Novum Testamentum
NTL	New Testament Library
NTTS	New Testament Tools and Studies
OPC	Oxford Philosophical Concepts
OSHT	Oxford Studies in Historical Theology
OTL	Old Testament Library
OTP	*Old Testament Pseudepigrapha*. Edited by James H. Charlesworth. 2 vols. New York: Doubleday, 1983–85
PPRT	Perspectives on Philosophy and Religious Thought
RB	*Revue biblique*
RRRCT	Ressourcement: Retrieval and Renewal in Catholic Thought
SGBC	Story of God Bible Commentary
SJSJ	Supplements to the Journal for the Study of Judaism
SPhiloA	*Studia Philonica Annual*
SPNT	Studies on Personalities of the New Testament
SRT	Studies in Reformed Theology
SVC	Supplements to Vigiliae Christianae
TBN	Themes in Biblical Narrative
TRS	Thomistic Ressourcement Series
WBC	Word Biblical Commentary
WUNT	Wissenschaftliche Untersuchungen zum Neuen Testament

Introduction

Heaven, hell, hope, and "the fate of every person who ever lived"—these are themes of the greatest consequence.[1] Will most human beings who have ever lived, as the ancient Jewish pseudepigraph 4 Ezra laments, ultimately end up condemned? Has God, from the foundations of the world, consigned some or most human beings to eternal damnation (or annihilation), as Augustine assumed, apparently consoling us with the notion that if this were not to redound to God's mercy, then it would at least redound to his power and glory?[2] Moreover, what would be the nature of this condemnation of human beings? Would they live forever in a state of conscious torment? And if so, what would be the nature of this torment? Would it be experienced as torment by those in this state; or rather, might such people have an eternal experience of the fleeting pleasures that occupied them in life, such a condition being seen as torment only by those who have taken hold of true, eternal life? Moreover, in this case, would the "torment" be simply the experience of a shrunken existence in the absence of God, or would it be the experience of the active, eternal punishment of God? If the former, how is creaturely existence sustained apart from the presence of God? If the latter, what is the nature of this "punishment"? Is it a purely punitive affair (with no other ultimate goal in view), or is it the unintended consequence of the collision between God's purgative love and the resolute impenitence of human beings?

Or perhaps the condemned either cease to exist at all, having been separated from the sustaining presence of God, or lead an ex-human existence, having rejected their nature as creatures made to reflect the goodness and justice of God. Another route, however, was taken at least as early as the first half of the third century CE, when Origen of Alexandria introduced the notion of *apokatastasis*, "restoration," the ultimate salvation of all human beings (and perhaps angels and all of created reality).[3] But the question comes: Can this account of Christian "universalism," or any other, simultaneously articulate a robust view of human freedom, or (better) of the distinct integrity of human agency? And what might all our hypotheses concerning what is sometimes called "individual" or "personal" eschatology tell us about God, humanity, divine agency, human agency, and their interrelationship?

These are the sorts of questions I am hoping to address in this book. But throughout the history of (especially modern) Christian thought, these questions too often have been addressed in one-dimensional ways—that is, scholars have tended to base their cases almost entirely *either* on Scripture *or* on theological Reason.* But few, if any, scholars have attempted to give due weight both to Scripture and to theological Reason.[4] Those emphasizing the role of Scripture usually have overdetermined the meaning of the

* By "Scripture," "Tradition," "Reason," and "Experience," I refer to the so-called Wesleyan Quadrilateral of theological authority. In my usage, "Scripture" stands for the canonical text of the Protestant tradition (though not much would be changed if we were working with the Catholic or Orthodox canon). "Tradition" stands for the major theological adjudications of the ecumenical councils (esp. Nicaea [325/381 CE] and Chalcedon [451 CE]) and the major figures and patterns of thought that have historically affirmed these adjudications. "Reason" stands for the God-given capacity to think and to speak "analogically" about God (on which, see immediately below). And "Experience" refers to the historical experience of the church across space and time, in which the worldview of the Christian faith has proven coherent and humanizing. The idea is that one needs all of these components for a holistic theological hermeneutic.

key texts and rejected any role at all for theological Reason.[5] By "overdetermined," I mean that such scholars have tended wrongly to assume that the relevant biblical texts directly address the specifics of the eternal destiny of distinct individuals.[6] On the other hand, the tendency of those who base their case primarily on theological Reason has been either to give Scripture little attention or to subscribe to a "theological hermeneutic," one of the features of which can be the relativization of the apparent original meanings of biblical texts.[7]

The story of this dichotomy in scholarship—Scripture versus Reason—is a long and complex one. But a rough summary might go something like this. Whereas many premodern interpreters of Scripture were not completely unconcerned with the original historical meanings of biblical texts, it is certainly the case that the rigorous attempt to locate biblical texts within their ancient, contingent contexts is largely a post-Reformation and post-Enlightenment development.[8] And it is this post-Reformation and post-Enlightenment environment that serves as the context for the hermeneutical developments in the Protestant tradition that have insisted on historical readings of Scripture over against those that would follow Scripture's reception in the premodern period. Indeed, as Protestantism's antipathy toward Tradition was combined with its failure to understand, and so to appreciate, classical Christian metaphysics, Protestantism grew naively overconfident about the extent to which the Bible alone could answer all of our theological questions.[9] And with the rejection of a philosophically thought-out metaphysic comes fideism; after all, theological Reason coordinates with and depends on a philosophical account of the nature of God, reality, and their relation. If you reject a philosophically thought-out metaphysic, then you ultimately reject the role of Reason in theology.

Given many Protestants' rejection of theological Reason, it is understandable that philosophically inclined scholars and Christians have been disinclined to countenance attempts to give an account of the theological role of historical-critical studies of Scripture. But what if we were to reject the false antithesis between a serious historical appreciation of the Bible and an appreciation of the metaphysics that resulted from the Bible's adaptation of Greek philosophical traditions? In other words, What if we were to countenance the possibility that a serious historical reading of the biblical texts that pertain to personal eschatology—that is, to heaven, hell, and hope—and an appreciation of classical Christian metaphysics are actually compatible? This book intends to argue that they should be recognized as such.

In summary, the following is the case that I will attempt to make. First, theological Reason, dependent on the *analogia entis* ("analogy of being")—that is, on the notion that God created humans with a capacity, however conditioned by finitude and corrupted by sin, to have some "natural" knowledge of himself—is an indispensable component of theology. In other words, through their God-given faculties of reason and logic, humans have a natural knowledge of God—namely, a knowledge that is not dependent on the saving revelation of God in Jesus and by the Spirit. By rejecting Reason, or natural theology, as a form of "epistemological Pelagianism"—as a knowing in which we merit knowledge of God rather than receiving it entirely passively as a revelatory gift that contradicts our nature—some have surrendered the very intelligibility of revelation and theology.[10] Put differently, by worryingly warding off anything that looks like the univocity of theological knowing and speaking, some have unwittingly subscribed to a total equivocity of theological knowing and speaking. If natural human knowing and speaking of God (i.e., Reason) bear no analogical relationship to God as he is, then a total equivocity of thought and speech results, and revelation and theology are rendered impossible.

Second, contra most accounts of eternal damnation and annihilation, although the New Testament presupposes the possibility of eternal loss, when we keep carefully in mind the rhetorical nature and ideal addressees of the relevant biblical texts, we see that the latter do not directly address specific questions concerning the eternal destiny of distinct individuals, as is usually supposed. Thus, when eternal damnationists, annihilationists, hopeful universalists, or dogmatic universalists adduce biblical texts as though some speak rather *directly* to the question at hand, they are overdetermining the biblical evidence.*

Third, contra some universalists, theological Reason, dependent on the *analogia entis*, does not dictate dogmatic universalism (or as Mats Wahlberg calls it, "necessitarian universalism"[11]). Rather, as I will argue in due course, while "necessitarian" or "dogmatic" universalists are right to reject elements of *libertarian* free-will defenses of the possibility of eternal damnation or annihilation, they are ultimately wrong to subscribe to a determinism in which a robust account of human agency is excluded.[12]

Fourth, as always in theology, we must sensitively read Scripture, humbly listen to the Tradition, carefully weigh the evidence of Experience, and rigorously attempt to make coherent metaphysical sense of the whole picture in light of Reason. When we do this, we will see that we must affirm the possibility of eternal loss while also simultaneously and emphatically affirming that (1) God is love and cannot but have good ultimate purposes for all that he creates (contra damnationist or annihilationist determinism); (2) Jesus died and rose for all people and for all of creation (contra limited atonement theory); and (3) if eternal damnation or annihilation is to be metaphysically coherent, it cannot be purely retributive but must consist of creaturely agency rejecting the eschatological embrace of God's love.

* "Eternal damnationists" refers to those who affirm the continuing, eternal existence of the eschatologically condemned. "Annihilationists" refers to those who maintain that the eschatologically condemned eventually cease to exist. "Hopeful universalists" refers to those who deem it appropriate, and perhaps even necessary, to long for the salvation of all people, even if they cannot dogmatically affirm such an outcome. And "dogmatic universalists" refers to those who positively affirm—on the basis of Scripture, Tradition, Reason, and Experience, or some combination of these—that all will certainly be saved.

I will make this case in three steps. First, we will concern ourselves with some theological prolegomena—namely, fundamental philosophical and theological commitments in the light of which alone the argument can be properly appreciated. Second, we will turn to Scripture itself, considering its witness to the question of individual or personal eschatology. Finally, we will conclude with some constructive proposals about what might be believed, taught, and preached about heaven, hell, and hope.

1

Preliminaries

Introductory Note

It will be easy for some readers, a couple of pages into this section, to wonder what any of this has to do with the topic of personal eschatology. So I will explain. As most defenses of the possibility of eternal loss (esp. eternal damnationism but also sometimes annihilationism) do not concern themselves much with philosophical and theological questions, and as most defenses of universalism do not concern themselves much with the original historical meanings of biblical texts, this section is necessary. After all, I am contending, against biblicistic accounts (which neglect or reject philosophy and theology), that theological Reason, dependent on classical Christian metaphysics, is an indispensable component of theology. But I am also arguing, against accounts in which the historical meanings of biblical texts are not taken very seriously, that classical Christian metaphysics is itself an "invention" (not de novo, of course) of scriptural revelation and that the historical meanings of the latter are foundational to theology, even though in this specific case (i.e., personal eschatology) Scripture is largely underdetermined. Thus, because I am affirming both (historical readings of) Scripture and theological Reason, it is necessary to provide an account of the nature and logic of this kind of theologizing.

How Theology Works

As I have already said, some will wonder why we should bother with theological Reason at all. Isn't Scripture sufficient? This brings us to the complex question of theological authority. In this regard, most Christian traditions have wanted to say that ultimate theological authority resides with the triune God himself and that this authority is, furthermore, uniquely embodied in the person and work of Jesus and then mediated by the Spirit through the Scriptures. But it is here that we encounter divisive questions. How can supreme theological authority reside with the triune God *in practice* if God's nature and character are decisively revealed in the historical particulars of a life attested to almost exclusively in the New Testament Scriptures? And what about natural theology? Is God revealed in the natural world in general (i.e., in "general revelation"), irrespective of the "special revelation" of the Scriptures? If so, in what sense, and how does this revelation relate to the way in which God is supposedly uniquely unveiled in Jesus, whose person and work are mediated by the Spirit through the Scriptures? Indeed, how did we get these Scriptures in the first place?

This is not the place to enter into all the details, but a brief summary statement is necessary. No one would be a Christian—and, hence, ascribe supreme theological authority to the triune God revealed in Jesus and mediated by the Spirit through the Scriptures—were it not for some kind of experience.[1] And this is what I mean by "experience," at least in this context. I am not necessarily talking about charismatic experience, though it does happen.[2] I am, rather, talking about experience in a much more general sense. Growing up after the Christ event (post ca. 33 CE), in a region exposed to the gospel message, and in a local community with both Christian churches and a churchgoing family is as much an experience as was Paul's Damascus road Christophany. One might go through the motions, as they say, within and for a culture or within and for a family, but one personally ascribes theological authority over the whole world and over one's own life only based on experience of one sort or another. And this is no less true of non-Christian worldviews and religious traditions.

But such "experience" is usually wanting of more clarity and exploration. In the Christian tradition, this further exploration focuses particularly on Jesus and the way in which he reveals the nature and character of the true God through the Spirit-inspired Scriptures. However, as most Christians recognize, we are not the first such people to embark on this journey. We stand, rather, in quite a long tradition. It reaches back now two thousand years—and, of course, Jesus himself insisted that it reaches back even further, through the covenant people of God and into the creative purposes of the one God himself.

But in terms of the revelation of God in the Christ event, we stand in a two-thousand-year-old tradition. Moreover, as most Christians recognize, the metaphysics of this tradition—that is, its account of the nature of (the triune) God and of God's relation to created reality in general and to the human being Jesus of Nazareth in particular—came to definitive expression in 325/381 CE and 451 CE with the Nicene Creed and the Chalcedonian Definition, respectively. I will say more about this in a moment. However, to be clear, when I say that the Christian tradition here came to some kind of *definitive* expression, I am not saying that the fourth century, rather than the early first, was when the true God was decisively unveiled; that the Nicene Creed represents all important Christian reflection prior to and contemporary with its penning; that the Nicene Creed is everywhere unambiguous and solves all of our theological problems; or that the Nicene Creed should put an end to all further theological reflection. Nor am I saying that the Nicene Creed replaces the theological witness of the Scriptures in general or of the New Testament in particular.

Indeed, it is precisely at this point that we meet a pervasive misunderstanding. What is the relationship between Jesus and the creeds, the New Testament and Nicaea, Scripture and Tradition—particularly as this concerns an overall account of theological authority? In this regard, many have assumed that, in the New Testament period, Christians were either unaware of or simply unconcerned with the sort of metaphysical reflections that were later enshrined in the creeds.[3] Moreover, so the argument goes, if they had been interested in these issues, they certainly would not have made any use of the Platonic tradition in order to explicate them.[4] However, as a number of scholars have recently argued, the opposite is actually the case. Indeed, evidence of a thoughtful christological adaptation of (Middle) Platonic metaphysics goes back as far as 1 Corinthians 8:6 (ca. 50 CE) and possibly earlier, finding particularly clear expression in John 1:1–18; Colossians 1:15–20; 3:10; and Hebrews 1–2.[5]

In this connection, the metaphysics of the Nicene Creed do not at all follow naturally or organically from ancient Greek metaphysical traditions and, actually, would never have reached their (Nicene) form without dramatic influence or adaptation from the outside.[6] In other words, so far from the Nicene Creed representing the victory of alien philosophical categories over the (unphilosophical) scriptural categories of the New Testament, it was actually the New Testament's christological adaptation of the Greek metaphysical traditions that generated Nicene metaphysics. Or to state it differently again, the early Christians—particularly Paul and the authors of the Gospel of John and the Letter/Homily to the Hebrews—"invented" Nicene metaphysics in order to make the claims they wanted to make about Jesus, about his relationship to God and to humanity and the rest of creation. Therefore, and this is the key point in this connection, to affirm the metaphysics of Nicaea (with their metaphysical and philosophical entailments) is simply to affirm—in a slightly more explicit form, of course—the metaphysics "invented" *ex Christi* (i.e., on the basis of Christology) by the earliest Christians.

It is nonetheless true, however, that Scripture's metaphysics are characteristically expressed narratively and thematically, not linguistically or philosophically, sometimes resulting in an underdetermined metaphysic. And indeed, it is on this basis that many have wanted to say that the technical metaphysics of Nicaea and Chalcedon represent inorganic developments away from the concerns of the New Testament. It is commonly claimed, "We don't need the later creedal tradition. Scripture is sufficient!" Of course, when the matter is put thus, how can one protest? After all, are we to say that Scripture isn't sufficient? Of course not. But the question arises: Sufficient in what sense and for what purposes?[7]

The answer to this question ought to be that Scripture is sufficient for that which it aims and claims to be sufficient. As far as the Old Testament goes, it is sufficient insofar as it aims and claims to tell the true "historical" and theological narrative of God and creation, of fall and election, of YHWH and Israel, of Torah and temple, of Torah fidelity and idolatry, of conquest, exile, and return. But of course, the Old Testament does not presume to provide an answer to a great many theological and practical questions. What, then, about the New Testament? Surely a robust biblical theology solves most of our problems, right? The New Testament is sufficient insofar as it aims and claims to tell the true "historical" and theological narrative of God, Jesus, and Spirit, of YHWH's return and the end of Israel's exile, of God's victory over the pagan gods, of the condemnation of sin, of the resurrection and the beginnings of new creation, and of the outpouring of the eschatological Spirit and the beginnings of God's new humanity. However, as was generally recognized from the early fathers to the rise of modern historicist biblicism, the New Testament raises a number of crucial questions for which it does not (at least explicitly) presume to provide an answer.[8]

Let us take five issues in this regard, all of which relate to one another and directly to our concerns: Chalcedonian two-natures Christology, open theism, theological passianism, the relationship between transcendence and immanence, and the so-called problem of evil. First, Chalcedonian Christology: Does the New Testament portray Jesus as fully divine, as uniquely intrinsic to and expressive of the one God of Israel? Yes.[9] Does the New Testament portray Jesus also as fully human? Yes. Does it portray him as some kind of hybrid being, a tertium quid who is neither properly divine nor properly human? No. A number of New Testament texts and traditions are emphatic that Jesus was and necessarily had to be fully human, the most famous of these texts being Hebrews 4:15: Jesus's humanity was and is "like ours in every way, apart from sin."[10] Both texts that emphasize Jesus's divinity and texts that emphasize his humanity have particular historical, scriptural, thematic, and theological logics, and neither emphasis seems designed to compete with or diminish the other.

But here we meet a puzzle that the New Testament itself does not show a great deal of interest in solving.[11] Some passages speak of Jesus "advancing in wisdom" (Luke 2:52). Others speak of his lack of omniscience (Mark 13:32 // Matt. 24:36) and his suffering. What are we to make of this in our attempt to hold New Testament Christology together as a whole (as the biblical authors themselves seem to want to do)? Should we conclude that the divine nature itself advances in wisdom, lacks omniscience, and suffers? After all, the relevant New Testament texts are not explicit about the two-natures distinction in these cases. What if we didn't bother with that distinction either? Would the theological consequences really be so devastating? Indeed, they would.

While open theism and theological passianism have had prominent proponents in the twentieth and twenty-first centuries, these positions represent deep metaphysical and theological misunderstandings and have devastating ramifications.[12] In an attempt to preserve the apparent meaning of a number of biblical texts—but perhaps, more importantly, to preserve a particular notion of creaturely free will—some theologians have felt the need to qualify classical notions of divine omniscience. On the view of open theism, God is not omniscient of the future but only of the past and the present. Indeed, the future does not yet exist to be known, even for God. Rather, like creatures, God does not transcend time but experiences time sequentially. On this view, to affirm God's knowledge of the future is necessarily to undermine any robust notion of creaturely freedom.

But this is to fail to appreciate that the doctrine of divine omniscience is simply an entailment of the doctrine of divine transcendence. In this regard, God does not know "the future." After all, from God's perspective, there is no such thing as "the future," a conceptual formulation that requires a contingent, sequential experience of time. If any such thing as the future existed from God's perspective, then God would have to be said to be growing, learning, and experiencing time in a way not very dissimilar to our experience. In this case, God's knowledge of the future would have to be conceived in terms of his infallible predictive abilities, based on his comprehensive knowledge of past and present reality. But again, this line of reasoning fails to appreciate that divine omniscience is simply one of the entailments of divine transcendence. Because God is the creator and not a creature, he does not experience contingent reality in the same way that creatures do. In other words, because he transcends time, he does not experience time in sequence as past, present, and future. Rather, it is precisely because he transcends time that he can be immanent and present to—and therefore omniscient of—all of what we call "time."[13]

As for the relationship between classical notions of transcendence and immanence and the question of creaturely freedom, I do not think that this is a problem either. The problem of competitive agency (i.e., God's sovereignty *or* creaturely freedom) is introduced only when we fail to properly appreciate the doctrine of divine transcendence—when we imagine that God and his creatures exist within the same order of being and in much the same way. But when we recognize their different ontologies—that God and that which is not God belong to different orders of being and exist in different ways—competitive agency is not even a possibility.[14] Indeed, it is a category mistake. To be sure, we may not be able fully and satisfyingly to express the relationship between divine and human agency, but we can at least say, in an apophatic sense, that hardline notions of radical determinism and radical free will are wrong. And they are wrong because they present God's agency and human agency as potentially in competition, thus compromising the doctrine of divine transcendence. In any case, the concept of creaturely freedom is notoriously slippery. We will return to it in the final chapter.

So what about theological passianism, the idea that God can experience suffering? Naturally, well-meaning Christians and even some prominent theologians—most notably, Jürgen Moltmann—have sometimes wanted to say that in the crucifixion God the Son somehow shares our suffering. However, to imply that the divine nature itself is susceptible to suffering is a mistake for at least two reasons. First, it places God in a creaturely relationship with time; second, it ascribes to him some kind of increase or growth in love and empathy. In this latter regard, it should be obvious that it would be theologically disastrous—however well intended—to ascribe to God a depth of love, compassion, and empathy in one brief moment in time that has not characterized him from all eternity. In other words, what a theological passianist tries to ascribe to God in one brief moment in time the classical Christian theist says has characterized God from all eternity.

Now we can consider two related topics: the way in which the biblical authors variously handle the relationship between transcendence and immanence and the problem of evil. In a sense, the polytheistic neighbors of the ancient Jews and early Christians had it easier on both fronts. One god—say, Zeus (a.k.a. Jupiter)—could remain transcendent, somewhat sovereign over the affairs of the *kosmos*, while other gods—say, Hermes (a.k.a. Mercury)—could be sent to accomplish divine immanence in this or that situation. Likewise, in terms of the problem of evil: one could say either that the gods are not particularly good or that some of them are and some of them are not—or, again, that some are favorably disposed to do this or that in a given situation and some are not. But what if you claim, as the ancient Jews and early Christians did, that there is only one God (in the full sense) and that he is simultaneously transcendent and immanent and infinitely good?

Taking the former point first: How could you think about, speak about, and depict this one God as simultaneously transcendent and immanent if you did not have the metaphysical category of omnipresence? The biblical writers employed various strategies: God's glory, name, wisdom, Word, Logos, spirit, and angels. Though these categories do more in Jewish and Christian texts than allow Jewish monotheists to vividly portray God's immanence without compromising his transcendence, they do not do less.[15] In this regard, we are not replacing, rejecting, or being unfaithful to the biblical witness when we speak of divine omnipresence. We are, rather, appreciating the accommodative nature of revelation (more on this in the next section). God inspired real historical people at real historical moments, with all the linguistic, conceptual, and theological resources they had, to reveal himself.

The same holds for the problem of evil. What we see in the biblical witness are various, essentially apophatic strategies: ways of trying to indicate what is most certainly not the case.[16] In Job's consideration of the problem of evil, the writer wants to clarify that (1) the evil that has befallen Job and his family is not *ultimately* attributable to God and that (2) evil, insofar as it is specifically associated with and perpetrated by the satan, does not represent a force with its own independent autonomy, such that God's ultimate sovereignty would be thereby undermined (and dualism would result). This is why evil is dissociated from God and associated with the satan, but it's also why the satan must ultimately ask God for permission to perpetrate it (Job 1–2).[17]

Of course, we might reasonably say that in solving a few philosophical and theological conundrums the writer of Job has also introduced a few. But we do well here to recognize the larger point being made: we experience deep evil but must not conclude that it undermines either God's goodness or God's sovereignty. Of course, Job does not even attempt to solve the philosophical and theological conundrum but, rather, offers a strategy for saying what at a minimum must be said. Thus, for example, when Augustine (354–430 CE) later famously and influentially postulated that there is no such *thing* as evil, he was neither rejecting nor replacing the theologizing of Scripture but, rather, recognizing therein strategies for saying precisely that: evil must be thought of more as a privation than as something possessing a positive ontological status. For if evil possesses a positive ontological status, it would seem ineluctably to follow that God *created* evil, which cannot be true.[18]

But for now, we ask, Does all of this not replace the theological authority of Scripture with the theological authority of the metaphysics of classical Christian theism? And is this not, thereby, simply to replace the authority of Scripture with the authority of certain emphases of the Platonic tradition? The historical situation is actually much more nuanced and interesting than this framing would suggest. As is well known, a thoroughgoing encounter between the Jewish tradition and Greek philosophy can be traced back as far as Aristobulus of Alexandria (ca. 181–124 BCE) and reached a full flowering in the Wisdom of Solomon (ca. 50 BCE) and the corpus of Philo (b. 25 BCE). And while these three examples hail from Alexandria, there is no particularly good historical reason to suppose that this encounter was confined to Alexandria. It is not surprising, therefore, that several scholars see a thoroughgoing confluence of Jewish wisdom and Greek philosophical traditions in several New Testament texts and traditions, not least the key christological texts of John 1:1–18; 1 Corinthians 8:6; Colossians 1:15–20; 3:10; and Hebrews 1–2.[19] However, as I am arguing elsewhere, these christological traditions appropriated Greek metaphysics neither unconsciously nor uncritically.[20]

Rather, the authors of these traditions adapted what they appreciated about Greek metaphysics *in order to make the claims they wanted to make about Jesus.*

They appreciated elements of Platonic metaphysics, including the notion of God (in their case, the God of Israel, YHWH) as the supreme good and originator of all that is, existing in the realm of being rather than in the realm of becoming (esp. John 1:1–14).[21] These authors adopted and adapted (Middle) Platonic intermediary doctrine to make a distinction at the level of the first principle, in order to speak of God (the Father) and the divine Logos (the Son).[22] They then affirmed, with John 1:14 most emphatically, that God the Son, remaining fully divine and belonging to the realm of being, assumed flesh and became fully human and a member of the realm of becoming, remaining ever after both fully divine and fully human, without confusion. There was, however, no wholly ready-made metaphysic with which, without serious adaptation, these early Christians could say what they wanted to say about Jesus. So they adapted what they knew of the ancient metaphysical traditions in order to make the claims they wanted to make about Jesus, thereby essentially inventing a new metaphysic.

No metaphysical tradition made distinctions at the level of the first principle, let alone *three* such distinctions, which is precisely what Nicene theology does. (Stoicism knew of no such distinctions, and Platonism and Gnosticism knew of hierarchies of principles.) No metaphysical tradition emphasized the necessarily noncompetitive relationship between God and that which is not God in the way that Chalcedonian Christology does. Therefore, though the Nicene Creed and the Chalcedonian Definition exhibit many elements of ancient Greek metaphysics, these elements have been adapted in order to say what the earliest Christians wanted to say about Jesus. It is thus not at all right to think of these creedal formulations as rejections or replacements of Scripture and scriptural authority. They are, rather, theologically authoritative metaphysical formulations in the light of which alone the revelational authority of the Spirit-inspired Scriptures makes coherent sense. One could also put it this way: the Spirit-inspired Scriptures draw Platonic metaphysics into the orbit of theological *and scriptural* authority, adapting these metaphysics as needed to serve their christological proclamation. Thus, for the question of personal eschatology, as for all other theological questions, we need theological Reason working with classical Christian metaphysics. And Scripture itself insists on this point.

How Revelation Works

But if God is immutable—that is, if God is transcendent, necessarily unaffected by the contingencies of created reality—how can God be said to reveal himself in and through created reality?[23] It is precisely at this point that many have misunderstood classical Christian metaphysics. Partly misunderstanding earlier Platonism and collapsing Platonism and Gnosticism, such critics contend, "This is just a way of keeping this Platonic God removed, separated from and untouched by the lesser (and corrupt and corrupting) ontology of created reality." However, even though this is largely a fair assessment of later Middle Platonic and certainly Gnostic metaphysics, this is emphatically not the point of classical Christian metaphysics.[24] In later Platonism and Gnosticism, the doctrine of divine transcendence entailed God's separation from the world. The only way this God could be said to interact with created reality was by means of various kinds or levels of intermediation.

In light of christological claims, however—that is, in light of the metaphysical claim that Jesus belongs fully and simultaneously, without confusion or separation, both at the level of the first (divine) principle and at the level of created, human reality—the early Christians were pushed to a radicalization of the doctrine of divine transcendence.[25] Somewhat paradoxically, but actually logically in terms of metaphysics, fully to affirm divine immanence in the full humanity of Jesus of Nazareth required a radicalization of the doctrine of divine transcendence in which it is precisely because God belongs to an order of being all his own (i.e., is transcendent) that he can be said to be fully and uncompromisingly present (i.e., to be immanent) in the full humanity of Jesus of Nazareth. Therefore, early Christians radicalized the Platonic doctrine of divine transcendence precisely so as to coherently articulate a robust doctrine of divine immanence in the created humanity of Jesus.

But for many Platonists, as for Gnostics, transcendence is simply "negative immanence."[26] In other words, to say that if the first principle is to "interact" with contingent reality it must do so via intermediaries is simply to conceive of the transcendence of the first principle in terms of its supremacy atop the chain of *the same order of being*. However, precisely because early Christians wanted to affirm that the highest principle (i.e., the true God) united himself to the full humanity of Jesus, without confusing or separating the divine and human natures, they were pushed to a radicalization of the doctrine of transcendence in which God belongs to an order of being all his own. In light of this doctrine of transcendence, it became intelligible to say that the true God united himself to the full historical humanity of Jesus of Nazareth, a union of natures without confusion or separation.

But in what sense can we say that this transcendent God reveals himself in and through the contingencies of created reality? Here revelation meets, as it were, two challenges: (1) the relationship between transcendence and immanence and (2) the brokenness of the *kosmos*, to which and within which God wants to reveal himself. We must always bear in mind, then, the necessarily accommodative nature of revelation.[27] And by "accommodative" I mean that for revelation to be revelation—that is, for God to succeed in communicating his nature and character to created (and broken!) reality—he must accommodate the revelation of himself to the linguistic, conceptual, and theological expectations and possibilities of the people to whom he reveals himself.

When God reveals himself to ancient Israelites, he accommodates that revelation to the presuppositions and expectations of those Israelites, however much the revelation also partly challenges, rebukes, and reconfigures those presuppositions and expectations. To say that God did not, or does not, do this is simply to say that he has never successfully revealed himself. The extent to which his revelation is "true" is determined by the extent to which it, within the constraints of the creaturely and broken context within which it came, analogically points to the nature and character of the triune God as he is.

But isn't the case with Jesus different? Actually, it isn't. Of course, the Christian tradition has always insisted on the full humanity of Jesus, but the theological entailments of this, particularly for a doctrine of revelation, have not always been appreciated. Jesus's first-century Jewish humanity made the sense that it made within the contingent constraints of his historical, linguistic, sociocultural, and theological context. To say that it did not make (or need not have made) the sense that it made in *this* contingent context is simply to commit docetism (i.e., to deny the full humanity of Jesus).[28]

In this connection, therefore, when we say that Jesus—the one person of the hypostatic union of the divine and human natures—is the decisive revelation of the true God, this does not mean that the Jesus attested to in the four canonical Gospels gives us the full and final answer to all of our theological questions. Indeed, when we read those Gospels well, we see that Jesus did not see himself or his vocation in terms of providing timeless theological truths. Rather, he saw his vocation as embodying Israel's God's defeat of evil and rescue of Israel and the world in and through his praying, preaching, teaching, exorcisms, healings, miracles, death, resurrection, ascension, and outpouring of the Spirit. In other words, the Jesus of the canonical Gospels was and is the definitive revelation of the true God in this specific sense: insofar as the triune God of creation had elected Israel to be his covenant people and had intended this covenantal relationship to be the means by which he would rescue Israel and the world, Jesus, as a first-century Jew *within this story*, perfectly embodied what it meant for both YHWH and Israel to be faithful to the covenant and thereby rescued Israel and the world.

Again, however, this point does not mean that the Jesus of the canonical Gospels gives us ready-made answers to all our theological questions. But this is no reason for epistemological or theological despair either. After all, Jesus poured out his Spirit and promised that it would guide his people into all truth (John 14:25–31; 16:4–15). Of course, this should not be taken as a summons to a thoroughgoing doctrine of "progressive revelation." The revelation of God in Christ ever remains the definitive revelation of the true God. However, we must always bear in mind the accommodative nature of revelation, even in this unique, christological case. The contingencies of history necessitate that more work, ever grounded in the person and work of Jesus and in the power of the Spirit, will need to be done.

A Historical-Critical Hermeneutic

There have always been many ways of reading Scripture Christianly. But in this book, I attempt to offer historical-critical accounts of the most relevant biblical texts—that is, accounts that try to take with utmost seriousness the so-called originally intended meanings of the texts within their historical contexts. Of course, this hermeneutical stance raises further questions. Is it metaphysically or theologically possible that God could have had intentions in mind that supersede whatever putative intentions the authors had in mind at the time of writing (such that we can discern a *sensus plenior*, or "fuller sense")? Couldn't the Spirit lead us into interpretations that are "on target" for particular persons or moments or contexts in subsequent history that have little to do with the apparent historical meanings of the texts (as allegorical and reader-response exegeses suggest)? Do canonical and creedal readings have no philosophical or theological justification?

To be clear, I am not denying a theological place for any of these (or other) reading strategies. But here I will attempt a post-Enlightenment, historical-critical reading of biblical texts, the underlying logic of which goes something like this: because God decisively revealed himself in the actual history of a Jewish human being in first-century Judaea, it is supremely appropriate for any attempt to understand this revelation to pay close attention to the meanings it might have had in that historical context.[29]

But this, too, raises further questions. At the hermeneutical level, should we treat all biblical texts the same, without discrimination? More particularly, if we are committed to a historical-critical hermeneutic of Scripture, what should we make of the fact that many biblical texts treat other biblical texts without much attention to what most historical-critical scholars would regard as the latter's range of probable historical meanings? In other words, if it can be demonstrated—as, in many cases, it can—that New Testament authors did not always treat Old Testament texts with utmost regard for their apparent historical contexts and meanings, does this not straightforwardly undermine the theological validity of a historical-critical hermeneutic? Why not simply treat Scripture the way these authors seem to treat the Old Testament?

These are complex issues that one cannot hope to sort out in short compass, but a few points need to be made. It is true that the New Testament—like Second Temple Jewish texts more generally—often treats Old Testament texts without the utmost concern for what seem to be their historical contexts and meanings. There is, however, a dialectic in this regard. The originally intended meanings of Old Testament texts exerted influence on audiences when these texts were written, and they have since existed in a mutually influencing dialectic with their Second Temple Jewish reception, a dialectic that has itself existed in a mutually influencing dialectic with the New Testament's reception. Simply because the New Testament does not always appreciate the putative historical contexts of Old Testament texts in the way that a historical-critical hermeneutic would appreciate the historical contexts of New Testament texts, it does not follow that a historical-critical hermeneutic is thereby automatically theologically invalidated.

In this connection, I would affirm what might be called a Christotelic historical-critical hermeneutic—as opposed to, say, a historical-critical hermeneutic that treats both testaments indiscriminately or a hermeneutic that, because the New Testament does not always appreciate the apparent historical meanings of Old Testament texts, assumes that we need not bother with the apparent historical meanings of New Testament texts. A Christotelic historical-critical hermeneutic does not treat the testaments indiscriminately either in historical-critical terms or in terms of a lack of concern for originally intended historical meanings. It recognizes, rather—against the former—that what is theologically authoritative is not the Old Testament as reconstructed by historical criticism (against the grain of the New Testament's reception of the Old) but, rather, the New Testament's reception of the Old. However, it also recognizes, against any suggestion that we need not concern ourselves with the potential theological authority of a historical-critical reading of the New Testament, that the New Testament itself claims that the story of God's dealings with the world and with Israel came to a decisive revelatory telos in real space-time-and-matter history, in the person and work of a real first-century Jewish human being. At the theological level, to insist on historical-critical meanings of Old Testament texts against the grain of their New Testament reception is to militate against the theological and christological message of the New Testament. And to insist that we should not concern ourselves with the historical meanings of New Testament texts because the New Testament does not always concern itself with the putative historical meanings of Old Testament texts is also to reject the message of the New Testament.

Conclusion

Christian theology is grounded in the decisive revelation of God in Christ, mediated by the Spirit through the Scriptures. But theological Reason, itself grounded in classical Christian metaphysics (i.e., the early Christian adaptation of the ancient Greek philosophical traditions), is also an indispensable component of Christian theology. As we will see in the next chapter, Scripture is somewhat underdetermined when it comes to the specific questions of personal eschatology. Thus—as we will see in the final chapter, and as is true of most theological and pastoral questions—it is necessary to make use of theological Reason to address the questions of heaven, hell, and hope.

2

Personal Eschatology *in the* Ancient Jewish *and* Christian Traditions

Introduction[1]

In what follows, it is not my aim to provide a comprehensive survey of biblical and extrabiblical eschatologies. Not only do such surveys already exist, but a comprehensive account of biblical and extrabiblical eschatologies would be necessary only if I were arguing that a careful historical-critical appreciation of all the relevant texts (1) stands directly in favor of eternal damnation, annihilation, or universal salvation; (2) stands directly against eternal damnation, annihilation, or universal salvation; or (3) indicates that some texts stand directly in favor of eternal damnation, annihilation, or universal salvation, whereas others do not, a case in which the strategy of *Sachkritik* (pitting one set of texts against another) might be employed.[2] However, my argument is precisely that the biblical evidence is not as interpretatively "determined" in this regard as is usually supposed.

Thus, my aim is as follows: to demonstrate that, while Scripture (particularly the New Testament) presupposes the possibility of eternal damnation or annihilation, the relevant biblical texts do not directly address the specifics of one's eternal destiny. In view of this aim, it has seemed necessary only to consider (1) some key texts that represent the main themes and emphases of biblical and extrabiblical eschatology and (2) the most relevant biblical texts for our reflections—that is, texts that seem to address personal or individual eschatology and are often taken as clearly damnationist, annihilationist, or universalist. We turn first to the pre-Christian Jewish tradition.

Personal Eschatology in the Ancient Jewish Tradition

The Tanakh (Old Testament)

Of course, any study of texts—the Tanakh, the Apocrypha and Pseudepigrapha, the Dead Sea Scrolls, Philo, Josephus, the New Testament, and so forth—requires one to situate the texts, as far as possible, within their putative historical contexts. In the case of the Tanakh, one would want to know about the ancient Near Eastern context in general and then, variously and depending on the probable date of the text or tradition in question, the Assyrian, Babylonian, Persian, or Greco-Roman context.[3] For our purposes, however, some general points will suffice.

With respect to personal or individual eschatology—that is, the question of the eternal destiny of distinct individuals—Bill Arnold nicely summarizes the Old Testament's (lack of) contribution to the question: "It can be said that Old Testament eschatology is not *primarily* individual eschatology in that it is seldom specific about the final fate of the individual as opposed to national or universal eschatology, which are often blended together in the Old Testament. . . . Also, it needs to be kept in mind that the Old

Testament has no fully developed conception of heaven and hell."[4] Indeed, the closest the Tanakh comes to addressing our question (and this isn't actually very close) comes in the late (i.e., ca. 164 BCE) text of Daniel 12: "At that time, Michael, the great prince, the protector of your people, shall arise. And there shall be a time of distress, the likes of which have never occurred since nations first came into existence. But at that time, your people shall be delivered, all of those found written in the book. Many who sleep in the dust of the earth shall awake, some to eternal life and some to shame and eternal contempt" (vv. 1–2).[5] The author here offers no sustained reflection or speculation on the point—only the bald claim that those found written in the book of life (i.e., faithful Israelites, from the author's perspective) will receive God's decisive eschatological "yes," while those not found written in the book of life will receive God's decisive eschatological "no" or "no more."[6]

The Hebrew word that I've translated as "eternal" in the above rendition of Daniel 12:2 is *ʿôlām*, and the Greek version uses the word *aiōnios*. Let's take a moment to consider the semantic force of these words in their historical contexts. The most detailed study is that of Ilaria Ramelli and David Konstan, who trace the use of the Greek *aidios*, *aiōnios*, and cognates from the pre-Socratics to Epiphanius, concluding as follows:

> We have seen that the term *aïdios* has its roots in the earliest Greek philosophical vocabulary, and more or less consistently refers to a strictly eternal stretch of time, without beginning or end, or at least endless. This use obtains in later pagan as well as Christian writers. The term *aiônios*, which seems to have been introduced by Plato and comes into its own in the Scriptures, is more complex: it may indicate a long period of time, or, in Platonizing writers, an atemporal or transcendental timelessness. Very broadly, *aiônios* corresponds to the uses of *aiôn*, which means a lifetime, a generation, or an entire age or epoch, particularly in Stoicizing contexts; in Christian writings, *aiôn* may refer to the temporal age prior to creation, to this present world, or, most often, to the epoch to come in the next

> world. *Aiônios* may also acquire the connotation of strict eternity, particularly when it is applied to God or divine things: here, the sense of the adjective is conditioned by the subject it modifies. There is also a technical sense in Christian theology, in which *aiônios* may refer more specifically to the *aiôn* that follows upon the resurrection but precedes the final reintegration or *apocatastasis*.[7]

It is certainly true that in ancient Jewish and early Christian eschatology, the semantic accent of *aiōn* and *aiōnios* (as well as of the Hebrew *ʿôlām*) falls on the qualitative rather than the quantitative (or atemporal) nature of time—as in the distinction between "this *aiōn*" and "the coming *aiōn*" (see, e.g., Matt. 12:32; Mark 10:30 // Luke 18:30; and Eph. 1:21), the former conceived as an unidyllic pre-eschatological reality and the latter conceived as an idyllic eschatological reality. But I am disinclined to conclude on this basis (contra Ramelli and Konstan) that the relevant condemnation texts (e.g., Dan. 12:2) that make use of *aiōn* or *aiōnios* should be taken to imply that a noneternal period of purgation will be followed by universal salvation. Such texts are simply not asking this question.

However, to contextualize our study of Second Temple Jewish texts and the New Testament, it is nevertheless important to trace the general lines of the eschatologies of the Tanakh. Two texts from Isaiah well represent some of the main themes and emphases:

> In days to come
>   the mountain of the LORD's house
> shall be established as the highest of the mountains,
>   and shall be raised above the hills;
> all the nations shall stream to it.
>   Many peoples shall come and say,
> "Come, let us go up to the mountain of the LORD,
>   to the house of the God of Jacob;
> that he may teach us his ways
>   and that we may walk in his paths."
> For out of Zion shall go forth instruction,
>   and the word of the LORD from Jerusalem.

He shall judge between the nations,
    and shall arbitrate for many peoples;
they shall beat their swords into plowshares,
    and their spears into pruning hooks;
nation shall not lift up sword against nation,
    neither shall they learn war any more. (2:2–4 NRSV)

A shoot shall come out from the stump of Jesse,
    and a branch shall grow out of his roots.
The spirit of the LORD shall rest on him,
    the spirit of wisdom and understanding,
    the spirit of counsel and might,
    the spirit of knowledge and the fear of the LORD.
His delight shall be in the fear of the LORD.

He shall not judge by what his eyes see,
    or decide by what his ears hear;
but with righteousness he shall judge the poor,
    and decide with equity for the meek of the earth;
he shall strike the earth with the rod of his mouth,
    and with the breath of his lips he shall kill the wicked.
Righteousness shall be the belt around his waist,
    and faithfulness the belt around his loins.

The wolf shall live with the lamb,
    the leopard shall lie down with the kid,
the calf and the lion and the fatling together,
    and a little child shall lead them.
The cow and the bear shall graze,
    their young shall lie down together;
    and the lion shall eat straw like the ox.
The nursing child shall play over the hole of the asp,
    and the weaned child shall put its hand on the adder's den.
They will not hurt or destroy
    on all my holy mountain;
for the earth will be full of the knowledge of the LORD
    as the waters cover the sea. (11:1–9 NRSV)

The story goes something like this. God created a beautiful world and set human beings, made in his image, over this world to steward it and care for it. But humans rejected God and thus became corrupt, together with the creation over which they were set. So God elected Israel to be the people in whom and through whom he would bring to fulfillment the plans he had had for Adam and Eve and for the whole creation. God would punish Israel for covenant infidelity and be present with them and through them during times of covenant faithfulness. Eventually, however, God would exalt Israel (or some subset thereof) to the position of world sovereignty that he had originally intended for Adam and Eve.[8] Therefore, the nations would one day flock to God, his temple, his land, his people, and his Torah, thereby either receiving eschatological condemnation or else abandoning their idolatry and joining in the eschatological blessings of Israel.[9] And this would necessarily issue in the renewal of all creation, symbolized not least in the harmony of the animal kingdom. Arnold again nicely summarizes the general nature of this Old Testament eschatology: "In it, the circumstances of history will be transformed but not transcended. The present cosmos, created as 'good' by Yhwh but temporarily marred by injustice, infirmity, war, and sin, and in general by evil will be reclaimed and redeemed by God. . . . This is no escapist eschatology, since it never completely forsakes the world we now inhabit. Rather it longs for, indeed expects, a period in which Yhwh triumphs over evil, redeems his people Israel, and finally rules the world in peace and salvation."[10] But again, there is no serious reflection on the eternal destiny of distinct individuals.

Second Temple Judaism

Interestingly, however, as soon as the Jewish tradition began to reflect deeply on personal eschatology we see the appearance of the so-called *misericordes* (i.e., the "merciful-hearted ones"). In this tradition, drawing on famous exemplars of intercession from Israel's Scriptures—Abraham on behalf of Lot and Sodom, in

Genesis 18:22–33, and Moses on behalf of the Israelites, following the golden calf episode in Exodus 32—various apocalyptic seers are depicted as appealing to God's mercy (as expressed in Exod. 34) on behalf of the damned (see esp. Apoc. Sedr. 5:7; 8:10; 16:12; Apoc. Zeph. 2:8–9; Gr. Apoc. Ezra [passim]; and 3 Bar. 16:7–8).[11] The most famous and poignant instance of this tradition comes in Pseudo-Ezra's protestations to the angel Uriel in 4 Ezra 4–9:

> I [Ezra] answered and said, "O sovereign Lord, I said then and I say now: Blessed are those who are alive and keep your commandments! But what of those for whom I prayed? For who among the living is there that has not sinned, or who among men that has not transgressed your covenant? And now I see that the world to come will bring delight to few, but torments to many. For an evil heart has grown up in us, which has alienated us from God, and has brought us into corruption and the ways of death, and has shown us the paths of perdition and removed us far from life—and that not just a few of us but almost all who have been created!" . . .
>
> I [Ezra] answered and said, "If I have found favor in your sight, show further to me, your servant, whether on the day of judgment the righteous will be able to intercede for the ungodly or to entreat the Most High for them, fathers for sons or sons for parents, brothers for brothers, relatives for their kinsmen, or friends for those who are most dear."
>
> He [Uriel] answered me and said, "Since you have found favor in my sight, I will show you this also. The day of judgment is decisive and displays to all the seal of truth. Just as now a father does not send his son, or a son his father, or a master his servant, or a friend his dearest friend, to be ill or sleep or eat or be healed in his stead, so no one shall ever pray for another on that day, neither shall anyone lay a burden on another; for then everyone shall bear his own righteousness or unrighteousness." (7:45–48, 102–5)[12]

By means of several further parabolic explanations, Uriel concludes to Ezra that, indeed, the number of the eternally saved will be few and the number of the eternally damned many. And though, of course, 4 Ezra does not offer a thoroughly metaphysical or philosophical explanation of the problem of creaturely sinfulness, the author does make what ultimately amounts to an apophatic claim: "For an evil heart has grown up in us" (7:48). In other words, whence the evil heart ultimately has come is not clear to the author, and he wisely chooses not to speculate. But he implicitly claims that the evil heart certainly did not come directly from God; therefore, God is not implicated in human sin.

In any case, in concert with 4 Ezra and, as we will see presently, the New Testament, most Second Temple Jews seem simply to have assumed the possibility of definitive eschatological condemnation (i.e., eternal damnation or annihilation; see, e.g., 1 En. 10:13; 48:8–10; 100:7–9; 108:4–7; Jdt. 16:17; 2 En. 40:12; 2 Esd. 7:26–38; 4 Ezra 7:26–38; 2 Bar. 59:5–12; 85:13; Ascen. Isa. 4:14–18; Sib. Or. 4:179–91; Josephus, *J.W.* 2.154–58 [on the Essenes], 162–64 [on the Pharisees]; *Ant.* 18.14–15 [on the Pharisees]). But this assumption was less a reflective doctrine about the eternal destiny of distinct individuals and more a general theological logic along these lines: God is good, therefore he will one day act decisively and irreversibly to eradicate evil and its perpetration.[13]

Personal Eschatology in the Early Christian Tradition

Jesus and the Gospels

As always, when we talk about Jesus, several critical caveats are in order. The four canonical Gospels variously but compatibly attest to the same figure.[14] As is well known, Mark, Matthew, and Luke—that is, the Synoptics—are much more similar to one another than they are to John. Mark is our first Gospel writer, with Matthew following first and appropriating Mark, then Luke following Matthew and appropriating both Mark and Matthew.[15] John is last of all, himself probably aware of all three earlier

Gospel texts and traditions.[16] The Synoptic Jesus is an apocalyptic prophet and—at least toward the end of his ministry—a messianic claimant who announces the arrival of God's saving rule on earth as in heaven. The Johannine Jesus is no less than this but also reflects deeply, and not infrequently, on his unique relationship to the one he calls "Father." All four Gospels, moreover, are ancient biographies and reflect—at least from our modern perspective—the typical historiographical "sins" of this ancient genre. They are happy to summarize, expand, truncate, and rearrange material as they see historically, theologically, or narratively fit.[17] In this regard, Matthew's and Luke's handlings of Mark are likely reasonably good guides to how Mark handled his sources.

In any event, in what follows I simply presuppose that the four Gospels are neither historically nor theologically irreconcilable (at a macro level); that in their different ways they bear an appropriate historical and theological relationship to Jesus as he was; and that, at the level of personal and ecclesial theology and praxis, we ultimately have to contend with the Jesus the four Gospels give us. This survey, moreover, will not feature a separate subsection on the Gospel of John, as this Gospel does not offer us any texts that should be considered in this regard (despite casual appeals of some proponents of universalism to, e.g., John 12:32).[18]

Mark

Let us begin with Mark. Like the other Gospels, Mark situates Jesus's ministry within the context of Jewish Scripture and the "narrative worldview" that this collection of sacred writings variously constructed for many first-century Jews.[19] The creator God, following the sin of Adam and Eve, had called Israel to be his special people; they would be the people in whom and through whom he would bring his saving presence to the world. But Israel had committed the same idolatry that characterized the pagan nations, and so the northern tribes were deported by the Assyrians (722 BCE) and then the southern tribes by the Babylonians (ca. 587 BCE). Israel had broken the covenant. As a result, as YHWH had always promised, he abandoned the temple and so left the temple and the land vulnerable to siege and destruction and the people vulnerable to exile.[20] And though many from the southern tribes had returned from Babylon following the edict of Cyrus (538 BCE), neither the northern tribes *nor God himself*, according to some Jewish texts and traditions, had ever properly returned.[21]

Indeed, the prophet Malachi had recorded these words of YHWH: "See, I am sending my messenger to prepare the way before me, and the Lord whom you seek will suddenly come to his temple. . . . Lo, I will send you the prophet Elijah before the great and terrible day of the LORD comes" (3:1; 4:5 NRSV). This is the context of the opening of Mark (1:2–3) and particularly of the entire ministry of John the Baptist, which in turn provides the context for Jesus's ministry.[22] (Indeed, Mal. 3 and 4 provide the introductory context for the public ministries of John and Jesus in the other Gospels as well.) John's baptism is a dramatic reenactment of the original entry into the promised land.[23] This would not have been missed by his fellow Jews and certainly not by Jesus himself.

In any case, after Jesus's baptism and messianic anointing by the Spirit (Mark 1:9–11), "the Spirit immediately cast [Jesus] out into the desert," Mark tells us, where he was "tempted for forty days by the satan, and he was with the wild beasts, and the angels were ministering to him" (1:12–13). In other words, so Mark is saying, immediately after receiving the Spirit's anointing for his messianic vocation—for the eschatological entry into the promised land to defeat the forces of evil and so to reclaim the land and the whole *kosmos* as sacred space—the Spirit cast Jesus into the desert to face the real enemy. And here we have an appropriation of extrabiblical traditions about Adam and Eve in the garden of Eden.[24] In these traditions—for example, the so-called Apocalypse of Moses and the Latin Life of Adam and Eve—the first human couple is said to enjoy harmony with God and with the rest of

God's nonhuman creation, until they succumb to the temptations of the satan/devil. Mark depicts Jesus, therefore, as succeeding where Adam and Eve had failed, as rejecting the satan's temptations and so restoring communion with heaven ("and the angels were ministering to him") and with the nonhuman creation ("and he was with the wild beasts"). Then Mark presents Jesus immediately thereafter as "preaching the gospel of God and saying, 'The time is fulfilled, and the kingdom of God has come near. Repent and believe in the gospel'" (1:14–15). This brief summary suffices for contextualizing the eschatological material in Mark's Gospel that most concerns us.

From here we move directly to the famous passage about the so-called unforgivable sin of blaspheming the Holy Spirit in Mark 3:28–30. Scribes from Jerusalem acknowledge that Jesus casts out demons, but they claim that he is capable of doing so only because he is possessed by their chief, Beelzebul (3:22). Having responded with the parable of the strong man, Jesus then says, "Truly I tell you, whatever sins and blasphemies human beings commit, all will be forgiven; but whoever blasphemes against the Holy Spirit can never have forgiveness, but is guilty of a sin with eternal implications" (3:28–29). Matthew's version offers even more clarity: "Therefore I tell you, all human sin and blasphemy will be forgiven, but blasphemy against the Spirit will not be forgiven. Whoever speaks a word against the Son of Man will be forgiven, but whoever speaks against the Holy Spirit will not be forgiven, either in this age or in the age to come" (12:31–32).

First, we have to remember the meaning of exorcism within the Gospel portraits of Jesus's kingdom-bringing work.[25] In the Gospels, as can be seen particularly in the placement of the temptation narratives directly after the messianic anointing (Matt. 3:13–4:11 // Mark 1:9–13 // Luke 3:21–4:13), the dark, demonic forces of evil are the real rival to Jesus's kingdom-establishing work. It isn't ultimately the Herodians, however undesirable some doubtless found them. It isn't ultimately the Romans, however much that pagan nation's rule embodied the real rival to Jesus's reign. According to the four Gospels, it is satan and the demonic forces of evil themselves that are the primary targets of Jesus's messianic "attack." Thus, for the Gospels, the spread of God's kingdom is *directly* connected to and effected by Jesus's exorcisms. Jesus does not kill a Roman; he casts out a demon. This is at the beating heart of the Gospels' interpretation of the evil that needs to be overcome for God's kingdom to be established in and through Jesus. In other words, to reject Jesus's exorcisms as acts of God's Spirit banishing the forces of evil and establishing God's kingdom is simply to reject God's kingdom.

Thus, when Matthew's Jesus says, effectively, that everything can and will be forgiven in God's kingdom—even a (temporary) rejection of Jesus himself ("Whoever speaks a word against the Son of Man will be forgiven," Matt. 12:32)—he makes it clear that this is, as we say, not petty and personal. Rather, to reject the exorcisms as the activity of God's Spirit establishing God's saving kingdom is ipso facto to reject that (kind of) kingdom. In other words, to say that someone—in this case, the Jerusalem scribes—can't enjoy forgiveness as long as they hold the opinion that the central evidence of the advance of God's kingdom is actually evidence of the chaos of satan's kingdom is to say something unremarkable. It's like saying, "So long as you stay in the darkness, you will not be in the light."[26]

Let us now turn to another text.

> He called the crowd with his disciples and said to them, "If someone wants to follow me, let them deny themselves and take up their cross and (so) follow me. For whoever wants to save their life will lose it, and whoever loses their life for my sake, and for the sake of the gospel, will save it. For what will it profit a person to gain the whole world and forfeit their life? Indeed, what might (such) a person give in return for their life? For whoever is ashamed of me and of my words in this adulterous and sinful generation, of them the Son of Man will also be ashamed when he comes in the glory of

> his Father with the holy angels." And he said to them, "Truly I tell you, there are some standing here who will not taste death until they see that the kingdom of God has come in power." (Mark 8:34–9:1)

This text comes roughly halfway through the Gospel of Mark and leads directly into the transfiguration scene (9:2–8). But what is Jesus saying? First, he is contrasting two ways of establishing God's kingdom on earth. One way, here assumed, is the way of force. It is the opposite of denying oneself and willingly taking up one's cross, which, in the first-century context of Roman Judaea, would have served as a graphic sign that one was precisely not interested in establishing God's kingdom by violent, revolutionary means. How, then, should we take the reference to the Son of Man—here clearly Jesus himself—being ashamed "when he comes in the glory of his Father with the holy angels" (8:38)? Many have taken this as a reference both to Jesus's parousia (i.e., "second coming") and to eternal condemnation at his arrival. The force of 9:1, however, makes this interpretation unlikely. Sometime in the early 30s CE, Jesus tells this crowd that some of them will *still be alive* when this whole thing happens. What is more, Mark—and, after him, Matthew (16:24–28) and Luke (9:23–27)—probably writing in the early 70s CE, records these words of his prophetic and messianic protagonist. How likely is it that Matthew, Mark, and Luke *all* record this prophetic prediction of Jesus if they also believed that, *forty or more years after the fact*, it still had not come to pass? Rather, it is much more likely that Jesus is talking about the relationship between two events that, from the perspective of the Synoptic evangelists, *had already happened*: the crucifixion and resurrection, on the one hand, and the fall of Jerusalem, on the other. In this case, this is what Jesus would be saying: if you do not choose the way of the cross, the way of peace, but rather the way of violent revolution, then you will be destroyed along with your people, your temple, and your land in the events of 66–73 CE—that is, of you the Son of Man will be "ashamed." Contrary to what is sometimes assumed or argued, then, this text does not directly address our concerns about the eternal fate of distinct individuals.[27]

We now turn to the only passage in which Mark refers to Gehenna:

> And whoever puts a stumbling block before one of these little ones who believe in me, it would be better for this person if a great millstone were hung around their neck and they were cast into the sea. If your hand causes you to stumble, cut it off; it is better for you to enter life maimed than to have two hands and to depart to Gehenna, to the unquenchable fire. And if your foot causes you to stumble, cut it off; it is better for you to enter life lame than to have two feet and to be cast into Gehenna. And if your eye causes you to stumble, rip it out; it is better for you to enter the kingdom of God with one eye than to have two eyes and to be cast into Gehenna, where "their worm never dies, and the fire never goes out" (9:42–43, 45, 47–48; cf. Isa. 66:24).*

What are we to make of a text like this? A couple of points need to be made. First, Jesus's prophetic warnings are characteristically hyperbolic. He does not really want people to cut off their hands and feet and to tear out their eyes (though the hyperbolic metaphor certainly trades on the fact that such literal punishments were then well known).[28] The point is that sinful humanity, as presently constituted, is not fit for God's kingdom, for God's new world. Indeed, in Paul's language, becoming fit for God's kingdom requires participation in Jesus's death, resurrection, and glorification via baptism. In other words, it requires nothing less than the reconstitution of our entire humanity. In Jesus's language, it requires the cutting off of hands and feet and the tearing out of eyes. In other words, becoming fit for Jesus's kingdom requires nothing less than the violent death of things that feel just as much a part of us as our own hands, feet, and eyes.

* Verses 44 and 46 are identical to v. 48 and, though they appear in some later manuscripts, are not found in the best, early manuscripts. Thus, they do not belong to the earliest recoverable form of the text.

But what about the warnings concerning Gehenna? *Gehenna* is the common English rendering of the Greek transliteration of the Aramaic phrase *gê hinnām*, derived from the Hebrew *gê hinnōm*, which means "Valley of Hinnom," a ravine to the south of Jerusalem. In several Old Testament passages (2 Kings 23:10; Jer. 7:31; 32:35; cf. 2 Kings 16:3; 21:6), the Valley of Hinnom is a place where Israelites are said to have grievously sinned by offering child sacrifice to the pagan deity Molech. In later Jewish tradition (e.g., 4 Ezra 7:36; 2 Bar. 59:10; 85:13; Sib. Or. 4:186), the Valley of Hinnom came to be associated with visions of fiery, eschatological judgment. It is in this sense that the term *Gehenna* is used by Jesus in the Gospels.[29]

That Jesus, therefore, believed in the possibility of eschatological condemnation is clear. But whether or not he reflected on the specifics of the eternal destiny of distinct individuals is not as clear.[30] The eschatology of the above text proceeds on this kind of theological logic: (1) God is holy; (2) God's new world will be charged with God's good-but-dangerous holiness (dangerous in the sense of necessarily consuming); thus, (3) one will need to be holy to be fit for God's new world. To be otherwise is necessarily to be cast into or to experience Gehenna.

It is not, then, that Jesus thinks he has come to die and rise only for certain people (as in limited atonement theory, on which see the footnote later in this chapter, under "Clearly Universalist Texts?"); that God cannot bring himself to forgive certain sins; or that there is no possibility of some people ever turning to the love of God. Rather, it is simply that one day God will flood the whole *kosmos* with his own presence and character—and it will take a particular kind of creature to endure that presence without being tormented or destroyed. We now turn briefly to Matthew's Gospel.

Matthew

As we turn to the other Synoptics, we will not cover material we sufficiently covered in Mark. We begin with Jesus's discourse about murder and anger from the Sermon on the Mount (5:21–26): "You have heard that it was said to those of ancient times, 'You shall not murder' and 'Whoever murders shall be liable to judgment.' But I say to you, everyone who is angry with a brother or a sister is liable to judgment; and whoever says to a brother or sister, 'Fool!' will be liable to the council; and whoever says, 'Idiot!' will be liable to fiery Gehenna" (5:21–22). This text provides an especially clear window into the hyperbolic nature of some of Jesus's eschatological rhetoric. Here, as elsewhere, Jesus intensifies what it means to be faithful to Torah.[31] Not only, Jesus says, will you be liable to earthly judgment if you murder someone, as the Ten Commandments have always stipulated, but even anger and insult will make you liable to judgment and to earthly councils. What is more, according to Jesus, calling someone an "idiot" could make you liable to fiery, eschatological judgment (i.e., Gehenna).

What, however, are the intentions of this rhetoric? Does Jesus mean to communicate that anyone who has ever uttered the word "idiot" at another person will literally be consigned to eschatological torment forever? Is this particular insult, in Jesus's view, *that* much worse than general anger or insult—which, at least as Jesus puts it here, only make one liable to earthly judgment? This seems extremely unlikely.[32] Rather, it is much more likely that this discourse is designed, like Jesus's eschatological discourse in general, to say that certain attitudes and behaviors (and the people who cling to them) are contrary to the character of the coming kingdom of God and that one should, therefore, expect them to be mercilessly condemned.

We now move to consider three of the most famous parables in all of Gospel literature, each coming near the end of Matthew's Gospel. First:

> Jesus answered, again speaking to them in parables and saying, "The kingdom of heaven may be compared to a king who gave a wedding banquet for his son. He sent his slaves to call those who had been invited to the wedding banquet, but they did not

> want to come. Again, he sent other slaves, saying, 'Tell those who have been invited: "Look, I have prepared my dinner, my oxen and my fat calves have been slaughtered, and everything is ready; come to the wedding banquet."' But they made light of it and went away, one to his farm and another to his business. But the rest seized his slaves, mistreated them, and killed them. The king was enraged. So he sent his soldiers to destroy those murderers and to burn their city. Then he said to his slaves, 'The wedding is ready, but those invited were not worthy. So go out into the main streets and invite whomever you find to the wedding banquet.' Those slaves went out into the streets and gathered all whom they found, both bad and good. And thus the wedding hall was filled with guests.
>
> "But when the king came in to see the guests, he noticed a man there who was not wearing a wedding robe, and he said to him, 'Friend, how did you get in here without a wedding robe?' And the man was speechless. Then the king said to the attendants, 'Bind his feet and hands and cast him into the outer darkness, where there will be weeping and gnashing of teeth.' For many are called, but few are chosen." (22:1–14)[33]

This is a remarkable parable about (1) Jesus's ministry and the surprising company he kept; (2) the coming judgment and salvation, focused on Jesus's death and resurrection and the destruction of Jerusalem; and (3) the nature of Jesus's kingdom (the wedding feast). The king (God the Father) is throwing a wedding banquet (the eschatological coming together of his Son and his people), and he has sent messengers (prophets past and present) to call all and sundry (with a particular focus on the chief priests and Pharisees, to whom Jesus directs this parable).[34] Most, however, have rejected the invitation—that is, Jesus and his vision of the coming of God's kingdom (including not least the kind of people that could and should be included)—and the king will come and burn their city as a result (a reference to the destruction of Jerusalem in 70 CE). In the end, the only guests that are welcome are those properly robed—a traditional sign of ritual purity.[35]

So what are we to make of this parable vis-à-vis our concerns about personal eschatology? Again, that Jesus believed in eschatological judgment—and, more particularly, that he saw the coming destruction of Jerusalem in 70 CE as an inauguration of the final judgment—is clear. But that it is hermeneutically appropriate to translate such a historically contingent parable about the events of 70 CE into a doctrine about the eternal fate of distinct individuals is not clear.

Next, let's have a look at one of the Gospels' most famous "Keep watch!" passages:[36]

> Then the kingdom of heaven will be like this. Ten bridesmaids took their lamps and came out to meet the bridegroom. Five of them were foolish, and five were wise. When the foolish took their lamps, they did not take oil with them; but the wise took flasks of oil with their lamps. As the bridegroom was delayed, all of them grew tired and slept. But at midnight, there was a shout: "Look, the bridegroom! Come out to meet him." Then all those bridesmaids got up and trimmed their lamps. But the foolish ones said to the wise, "Give us some of your oil, because our lamps are going out." But the wise answered and said, "No! There will not be enough for us and for you; instead, go to the dealers and buy some." And when they departed to buy some, the bridegroom came, and those who were prepared entered with him to the wedding banquet; and the door was shut. After this, the rest of the bridesmaids came also and said, "Lord, lord, open to us." But answering, he said, "Truly I tell you, I do not know you." Keep awake, therefore, because you know neither the day nor the hour. (25:1–13)

In a sense, the message of this parable is rather straightforward. While the passage has the fall of Jerusalem in 70 CE immediately in view, Jesus, as I stated above, sees this event as the inauguration and model of the eschatological denouement. Jesus is saying, a moment will come when God's eschatological future will collide with your present humanity. And in terms of the moral constitution of your character, you will want to be as ready for that moment as possible.

Finally, we turn to what is probably the most famous eschatological parable in the Gospels, at least as it pertains to the eschatological destinies of human beings:[37]

> When the Son of Man comes in his glory, and all the angels with him, then he will sit on his glorious throne. And all the nations will be gathered before him, and he will separate people one from another as a shepherd separates the sheep from the goats, and he will place the sheep at his right hand and the goats at his left. Then the king will say to those at his right hand, "Come, you who are blessed by my Father, inherit the kingdom prepared for you from the foundation of the world; for I was hungry and you gave me food, I was thirsty and you gave me something to drink, I was a stranger and you welcomed me, I was naked and you clothed me, I was sick and you looked after me, I was in prison and you visited me." Then the righteous will answer him and say, "Lord, when did we see you hungry and feed you, or thirsty and give you something to drink? And when did we see you as a stranger and welcome you, or naked and clothe you? And when did we see you sick or in prison and visit you?" And answering, the king will say to them, "Truly I tell you, just as you did it to one of the least of these who are members of my family, you did it to me."[38] Then he will also say to those at his left, "Depart from me, you that are cursed, into the eternal fire prepared for the devil and his angels; for I was hungry and you gave me no food, I was thirsty and you gave me no drink, I was a stranger and you gave me no welcome, naked and you gave me no clothing, sick and in prison and you paid me no visit." Then they also will answer and say, "Lord, when did we see you hungry or thirsty or a stranger or naked or sick or in prison and did not take care of you?" Then answering, he will say to them, "Truly I tell you, just as you did not do it to

> one of the least of these, you did not do it to me." And these will depart to eternal punishment, but the righteous to eternal life." (25:31–46)

The first thing to note here is that, in context, the parable is about what we tend to call social justice—that is, it is about food, water, clothes, and hospitality. The second thing to note is that it is specifically about the way in which people have treated members of the Christian community (25:40: "Truly I tell you, just as you did it to one of the least of these who are members of my family, you did it to me").[39] In other words, the sheep and the goats do not represent a general division of all humanity (e.g., non-Christians and Christians, or supposed Christians and genuine Christians) but a specific division of non-Christian humanity. The parable teaches that those who serve Jesus's people in concrete ways thereby (even if unwittingly) serve Jesus himself. And they will, therefore, receive their positive eschatological reward, *whether they ever had any intention of being a follower of Jesus or not*. In any case, it should be clear that to attempt to directly translate this passage into a doctrine about the eternal fate of distinct individuals is hermeneutically inappropriate.

We now turn to a classic text in Luke's Gospel.

Luke

Since a consideration of Luke's version (14:15–24) of the banquet parable (Matt. 22:1–14) would not add materially to our considerations, we turn directly to the famous parable of the rich man and Lazarus. Jesus says,

> There was a certain rich man, clothed in purple and fine linen and feasting sumptuously every day. And there was a certain poor man by the name of Lazarus, covered in sores, who laid at his gate, longing to satisfy his hunger with what fell from the rich man's table—even the dogs would come and lick his sores! But it came

> about that when the poor man died, he was carried by angels to Abraham's bosom. The rich man also died and was buried. And in Hades, lifting up his eyes in his torments, he saw Abraham far away, and Lazarus was in his bosom. He called out, "Father Abraham, have mercy on me and send Lazarus to dip the tip of his finger in water and cool my tongue; for I am in agony in these flames." But Abraham said, "Child, remember that you received good things during your lifetime, and Lazarus in his lifetime evil things; but now he is comforted here, and you are in agony. And in any case, between us and you a great chasm has been fixed, so that those who might want to pass from here to you cannot do so; nor can anyone cross from there to us." He said, "I beg you, then, Father, to send him to my father's house—for I have five brothers—so that he might warn them, in order that they will not also come into this place of torment." Abraham replied, "They have Moses and the prophets; let them listen to them." He said, "No, Father Abraham; but if someone goes to them from the dead, they will repent." He said to him, "If they do not listen to Moses and the prophets, neither will they be convinced even if someone rises from the dead." (16:19–31)

Jesus offers this parable to the Pharisees and scribes (15:1–2; 16:14), and it comes, within the literary (and therefore interpretative) context of Luke's Gospel, closely on the heels of the so-called parable of the prodigal son (15:11–32). And one of the main points of the latter parable, which is also addressed to the Pharisees and scribes (15:1–2), is that in the ministry of Jesus God is welcoming unlikely people into the kingdom (15:1: "the tax collectors and sinners who were coming near to listen to him"). In this connection, we can quote Jesus himself: "I did not come to call the 'righteous' but sinners to repentance" (5:32). Of course, in the ministry of Jesus, God is also happy to welcome traditionally faithful Jews (not least the Pharisees—i.e., the elder brother in the parable), should they join Jesus's movement and welcome those he welcomes (i.e., the prodigal son).

This is also the interpretative context of the above-mentioned parable in Luke 16. Its stark picture of eschatological reversal is typical of Luke's style and theology. Note, for instance, the blunt reversal reflected in Mary's Magnificat:

> He has brought down the mighty from their thrones
> and exalted the lowly;
> he has filled the hungry with good things
> and sent the rich away empty. (1:52–53)[40]

And this latter note of economic criticism, which is characteristic of Luke and, of course, prominent in the above parable, is picked up just before the introduction of this parable and associated with the primary target of Jesus's critique: "'No slave can serve two masters, for the slave will either hate the one and love the other or be devoted to the one and despise the other. You cannot serve God and money.' The Pharisees, who loved money, heard all these things and ridiculed him" (16:13–14).[41]

In this parable, therefore, the rich man represents a Pharisee—someone many Jews would have supposed to be as securely internal to the faithful people of God as any Israelite could hope to be. Lazarus, the poor man, represents the tax collectors and sinners, whose welcome the Pharisees begrudge. Surely, Luke's Pharisees think, these tax collectors and sinners are not proper recipients of the eschatological welcome Jesus is giving them. But surely, Luke's Pharisees also think, they themselves are proper members of the people of God and in good covenant standing. This is the presumed context of the rich man's triple appeal to "Father Abraham" (16:24, 27, 30) and of the striking way in which Lazarus's eschatological state and location are twice described: the bosom/lap of Abraham (16:22, 23).[42] With Luke's characteristic economic concerns (here particularly associated with the Pharisees) and in his stark imagery of eschatological reversal, he ironically implies that those who presently think they are Abraham's children par excellence (i.e., scrupulously Torah-faithful Israelites in good covenant standing) might find themselves eschatologically separated from the patriarch, desperately and ineffectually calling across a great chasm, "Father Abraham!"[43] On the other hand, those whom the Pharisees think are and should be excluded from God's eschatological kingdom (the tax collectors and sinners Jesus welcomes) might be safe and secure in Abraham's eschatological embrace. It all depends on one's response to Jesus.

But this is not, of course, a piece of systematic eschatology. It is, rather, a pointed statement about what Jesus is doing in the present: insofar as you reject the tax collectors and sinners Jesus welcomes into the kingdom of Israel's God and into the family of Abraham's children, you will be seen to have been on the wrong side of eschatological history. But it should be obvious that this Gospel text is not directly translatable into a doctrine about the eternal destiny of distinct individuals. With that having been said, it is now time to turn to Paul the apostle.

Paul

To understand Paul's eschatology, it is important to first grasp the logic of his macrotheological vision.[44] This vision can be glimpsed in several key passages. It is tersely and famously stated in Romans 8:29: "For those whom he foreknew he also predestined to share the same form as the image of his son, so that he might be the firstborn among many brothers and sisters." It is presupposed and expressed in different ways when Paul speaks of ultimately being conformed to the image of the resurrected and glorified Jesus in 1 Corinthians 15:20–58, 2 Corinthians 3:18, Ephesians 4:23–24, and Colossians 3:10 (with Col. 1:15), or when Paul speaks of ultimately attaining to the resurrection and thereby to a body like "[Jesus's] glorious body" (Phil. 3:21). This macrotheological vision is also presupposed and expressed in longer units across Paul's letters, not least of which are Romans 1–8 and Philippians 2:6–3:21.

Reasoning in christological and teleological retrospect, and reprising the whole account of creational theology from Genesis 1–2, Paul's vision goes like this: In the beginning, God created Adam and Eve in the image of the preexistent Son and toward the telos of growing into the fullness of the incarnate, crucified, resurrected, and glorified Jesus.[45] Thus God had always intended to steward his *kosmos* through humans patterned after the image of his incarnate, crucified, resurrected, and glorified Son.[46]

For Paul's eschatology, then, two things are of particular importance, and they are themselves intimately related: the *constitution* and the *character* necessary to steward God's world in God's way. Several passages could illustrate the first point, but 1 Corinthians 15 is perhaps the most obvious. Paul argues that only those with a *sōma pneumatikon* (a "body transformed, energized, and sustained by the Spirit"), which bears the image of the "second human from heaven," will be able to "inherit God's kingdom" (15:44–50). After all, simple "flesh and blood are not able to inherit God's kingdom" (15:50). For our purposes, it is not necessary to get into the debates about the phrase *sōma pneumatikon*—that is, whether it refers to a body wholly composed of spirit (perhaps in terms of the material *pneuma* of Stoicism) or to a body only energized by (but not wholly composed of) spirit.[47] What matters is that Paul is talking about a creature's *constitution*. Only a certain kind of ontology can exist in God's space. A similar point could be made from other passages in Paul, not least of which are Romans 8 and Philippians 3:20–21.[48]

With respect to the second feature of Paul's eschatology that I would highlight in this connection—that, in addition to a particular constitution, humans require a particular *character* to steward God's world in God's way—two passages illustrate the point well. In Galatians 5:19–23, when considering the kind of people who will "inherit God's kingdom" (i.e., steward God's new creation), Paul rules out some character traits and enjoins others: "Now the works of the flesh are clear, which are sexual immorality, impurity, licentiousness, idolatry, sorcery, enmities, strife, jealousy, outbursts of anger, quarrels, dissensions, factions, envy, drunkenness, carousing, and things like these—that which I am warning you about, about which I warned you before. Those who do such things will not inherit God's kingdom. But the fruit of the Spirit is love, joy, peace, patience, kindness, generosity, faithfulness, gentleness, and self-control. Against such things there is no law." In other words, God's kingdom, God's new creation, will be suffused through and through by the character of God himself. Because of this, certain character traits are simply ruled out.

Another angle of vision comes in 1 Corinthians 6. Paul rebukes the Corinthian Christians for taking intracommunal legal disputes to secular authorities in Corinth: "A certain one of you, having a grievance against another—Does such a person dare to take it to court before the unrighteous rather than the saints? Or do you not know that the saints will judge the *kosmos*? And if the *kosmos* is to be judged by you, are you unworthy to try trivial cases? Do you not know that we will judge angels—to say nothing of ordinary matters?" (6:1–3). In other words, because glorified human beings will steward (i.e., judge) God's new world, and because, in Paul's inaugurated eschatology, those in Christ should be anticipating this role in the present, to pretend as though justice can be properly administered outside of the Christian community is to reject what God has done, is doing, and will do. This is the context of 1 Corinthians 6:9–10: "Do you not know that wrongdoers will not inherit the kingdom of God? Do not be deceived! Fornicators, idolaters, adulterers, male prostitutes, sodomites, thieves, the greedy, drunkards, revilers, robbers—none of these will inherit the kingdom of God." This is the point: one day you will steward God's new world (i.e., inherit the kingdom of God), and it will take a particular kind of moral constitution to do so in God's way.[49]

In this subdivision, I want to consider two more Pauline texts. The first is 2 Thessalonians 1:5–10:

> This is proof of God's righteous judgment and is intended to make you worthy of God's kingdom, for which you are also suffering. For it is just of God to repay with affliction those who afflict you and to give relief with us to you who are afflicted, when the Lord Jesus is revealed from heaven with his mighty angels in flaming fire, inflicting vengeance on those who do not know God and on those who do not obey the gospel of our Lord Jesus. These will suffer the just punishment of eternal destruction, separated from the presence of the Lord and from the glory of his might, when he comes to be glorified by his saints and marveled at on that day among all who have believed, because our testimony to you was believed.

The key to an eschatological text like this is to appreciate the context and the ideal addressees of the eschatological warnings. The Thessalonian church had endured "persecutions" (2 Thess. 1:4; cf. 1 Thess. 1:6–7; 2:14; 3:3–5), and Paul had interpreted these persecutions as attempts of the dark, suprahuman forces of evil (1 Thess. 2:18: "the satan"; 3:5: "the tempter") to destroy the Thessalonian church and thus to render Paul and his associates' labors "futile" (1 Thess. 3:5).

Though Paul possibly hints at this context in 1 Thessalonians 2:16, in 2 Thessalonians 2:1–12 he further specifies the particular human instrument(s) of "the working of the satan" (2:9): "the lawless one" who "opposes and exalts himself above every so-called god or object of worship, so that he takes his seat in the temple of God, declaring himself to be God" (2:3–4 NRSV). This almost certainly refers to the historical event of Gaius Caligula, Roman emperor from 37 to 41 CE, attempting to install a cult statue of himself in the guise of the Greco-Roman chief deity Zeus (Jupiter) in the Jerusalem temple (41 CE).[50] This action drew sharp and horrified criticism from many Jewish quarters, not only because it represented a profanation of the imageless Jerusalem temple but also because it evoked a similar incident involving Antiochus Epiphanes IV, the Seleucid king whose attempt (inter alia) to install a cult statue of himself in the guise of Zeus had provoked the Maccabean revolt roughly two centuries earlier.

With respect to Caligula's actions, the influential Jewish philosopher Philo of Alexandria wrote an entire book, *Embassy to Gaius*, detailing his attempt to dissuade the emperor from proceeding with the plan. And the first-century Jewish historian Josephus writes, "The insolence with which the emperor Gaius defied fortune surpassed all bounds: he wished to be considered a god and to be hailed as such, he cut off the flower of the nobility of his country, and his impiety extended even to Judaea. In fact, he sent Petronius with an army to Jerusalem to install in the sanctuary statues of himself; in the event of the Jews refusing to admit them, his orders were to put the recalcitrants to death and to reduce the whole nation to slavery."[51]

This is the historical context of the above passage about fierce eschatological condemnation at Jesus's return (2 Thess. 1:5–10). Like John the Revelator and doubtless many other Jews and Christians, Paul perceived the dark workings of the satan in the divine pretensions of pagan kings, their gods, and their oppressive empires. These pagan kings and their empires represented and embodied the dark, demonic forces of evil against which Paul's proclamation of the advancing kingdom of Jesus most set itself. One day, Paul believed, the Lord Jesus himself would say a fierce, decisive, and irreversible no to this kind of demonic activity and to its imperial conduits.

Let us now turn briefly to a statement of Paul's in 1 Corinthians 15:29 that catches most readers unawares: "Otherwise, what will those people do who receive baptism on behalf of the dead? If the dead are not raised at all, why are people baptized on their behalf?" Unsurprisingly, this text has been the subject of no small amount of debate.[52] But in my view, the meaning of 1 Corinthians

15:29 should not be much in doubt, given the illuminating tradition found in 2 Maccabees 12:32–45:

> After the festival called Pentecost, they [Judas Maccabeus and his army] hurried against Gorgias, the governor of Idumea, who came out with three thousand infantry and four hundred cavalry. When they joined battle, it happened that a few of the Jews fell. . . . As Esdris and his men had been fighting for a long time and were weary, Judas called upon the Lord to show himself their ally and leader in the battle. In the language of their ancestors he raised the battle cry, with hymns; then he charged against Gorgias's troops when they were not expecting it, and put them to flight.
>
> Then Judas assembled his army and went to the city of Adullam. As the seventh day was coming on, they purified themselves according to the custom, and kept the sabbath there.
>
> On the next day, as had now become necessary, Judas and his men went to take up the bodies of the fallen and to bring them back to lie with their kindred in the sepulchers of their ancestors. Then under the tunic of each one of the dead they found sacred tokens of the idols of Jamnia, which the law forbids the Jews to wear. And it became clear to all that this was the reason these men had fallen. So they all blessed the ways of the Lord, the righteous judge, who reveals the things that are hidden; and they turned to supplication, praying that the sin that had been committed might be wholly blotted out. The noble Judas exhorted the people to keep themselves free from sin, for they had seen with their own eyes what had happened as the result of the sin of those who had fallen. He also took up a collection, man by man, to the amount of two thousand drachmas of silver, and sent it to Jerusalem to provide for a sin offering. In doing this he acted very well and honorably, taking account of the resurrection. For if he were not expecting that those who had fallen would rise again, it would have been superfluous and foolish to pray for the dead. But if he was looking to the splendid reward that is laid up for those who fall asleep in godliness, it was a holy and pious thought. Therefore he made atonement for the dead, so that they might be delivered from their sin. (NRSV)

In this instance, Judas Maccabeus's troops had died immediately after (and because of) committing idolatry. However, Judas and his men hoped that prayers and financial contributions for atonement offerings on their behalf might redound to their eschatological benefit. And it looks as though, mutatis mutandis, the Corinthians' acts of baptism on behalf of the dead served a similar purpose. Of course, there are still unanswered questions with respect to 1 Corinthians 15:29: Does "the dead" refer to departed Corinthian Christians in general, Corinthian Christians who have departed in a state that some consider to be sinful, people who have never heard the gospel (family, friends, etc.), or all of the above and others? Moreover, we cannot be sure how widespread this practice was in ancient Judaism or early Christianity.

For our purposes, however, what principally matters is the following: Some Corinthian Christians were baptized on behalf of the dead, and Paul does not directly challenge this practice. And this tells us that, for all of Paul and early Christianity's proper emphasis on a judgment according to each individual's works (see esp. Rom. 2:6; 2 Cor. 5:10; and Gal. 6:5), they were also capable of holding this together with a notion of a shared, communal faithfulness. At the very least, then, a text like this challenges the overly individualistic notion that a person's individual moral track record is the whole eschatological story.

Hebrews and the Catholic Epistles

We now turn to Hebrews and the so-called Catholic Epistles, a few of which contain material relevant for our purposes. We'll begin with Hebrews:

> Therefore, leaving behind the rudimentary teaching about Christ, let us move on toward perfection, not laying again the foundation: repentance from dead works and faithfulness toward God, instruction about baptisms, laying on of hands, resurrection of the dead, and eternal judgment. And this we will do, if God permits.

> For it is impossible to restore again to repentance those who have once been enlightened, and have tasted the heavenly gift, and have become partakers of the Holy Spirit, and have tasted the goodness of the word of God and the powers of the age to come, and then have fallen away, since for themselves they are recrucifying the Son of God and holding him up to contempt. Ground that drinks up the rain that frequently falls on it and that produces a crop useful to those for whom it is cultivated receives a blessing from God. But if it bears thorns and thistles, it is worthless and near to being cursed; its end is to be burned.
>
> But I am confident in your case, beloved, of better things, things that have to do with salvation—even if we speak in this way. For God is not unjust so as to overlook your work and the love that you demonstrated for his name's sake when you served the saints, as you still do. And we want each of you to show the same diligence so as to realize the full assurance of hope to the end, so that you might not be sluggish but, rather, imitators of those who through faith and patience inherit the promises. (Heb. 6:1–12)

This text has long been at the heart of contentious debates about the doctrine of "perseverance"—about whether or not the New Testament envisages the possibility that someone can receive the Holy Spirit, participate in Christian community, and then reject the Spirit and the Christian community and thereby the prospect of eternal salvation.[53] Here I only make a few points. First, this text belongs with other warnings in the New Testament (esp. Matt. 12:43–45 // Luke 11:24–26; 2 Pet. 2:20–21) that those who have received the gospel—and who, therefore, "know better"—will be more culpable for having later rejected the gospel than those who have never received it. Second, this passage means what it means in relation to Hebrews's thoroughgoing appropriation of the wilderness typology with respect to the present generation of Christians: in a sense, they have been decisively rescued from Egypt but still must persevere in and through the wilderness so as not to fall away like that first generation (cf. 1 Cor. 10:1–22). Third, though falling away (apostasy) is held out as a hypothetical possibility (not as a given fact, as in 2 Pet. 2:17–21), its likelihood is immediately rejected by the author (Heb. 6:9). And fourth, though phrases like "being cursed" and "its end is to be burned" certainly reflect the condemnatory language of Jewish eschatology, to say that here we have serious reflection about the eternal fate of distinct individuals would be to go beyond the evidence.[54]

Now let's consider a few passages from 1 and 2 Peter:

> For Christ also suffered for sins once for all, the righteous for the unrighteous, in order to bring you to God. He was put to death in the flesh but made alive by the Spirit,[55] in which also he went and made a proclamation to the spirits kept under guard, who in former times did not obey, when God waited patiently in the days of Noah, when the ark was constructed, in which a few—that is, eight persons—were saved through water. And baptism, which this prefigured, now saves you—not as a removal of dirt from the body but as an appeal to God for a good conscience, through the resurrection of Jesus Christ, who is at the right hand of God, having gone into heaven and made all angels, authorities, and powers subject to him. . . .
>
> For this is the reason the gospel was proclaimed even to the dead, so that, though they had been judged in the flesh as human beings are judged, they might live in the spirit as God does. (1 Pet. 3:18–22; 4:6)

> For if God did not spare the angels when they sinned, but committed them to chains of deepest darkness in Tartarus to be kept until the judgment; and if he did not spare the ancient world, even though he saved Noah, a herald of righteousness, with seven others, when he brought a flood on a world of the ungodly; and if by turning the cities of Sodom and Gomorrah to ashes he condemned them to extinction, having made them an example of what is coming to the ungodly; and if he rescued Lot, a righteous man distressed by the licentiousness of the lawless (for by what he saw and heard, that righteous man, living among them day after day, was tormented in his righteous soul by their lawless deeds), then

> the Lord knows how to rescue the godly from trial and how to keep the unrighteous under punishment until the day of judgment—not least those who indulge the flesh with defiling lust and who despise authority. . . .
>
> This is now, beloved, the second letter I am writing to you. In these I am trying to arouse your sincere intention by reminding you to remember the words spoken beforehand by the holy prophets, and the commandment of the Lord and savior spoken through your apostles. First of all, you must appreciate this: in the last days, scoffers will come, scoffing and indulging their own lusts and saying, "Where is the promise of his coming? For ever since our ancestors died, all things continue as they were from the beginning of creation!" For they deliberately ignore this point: that by the word of God the heavens existed long ago and an earth was established out of water and by means of water, because of which the *kosmos* of that time was flooded with water and perished. But by the same word, the present heavens and earth have been reserved for fire, being kept until the day of the judgment and destruction of the ungodly.
>
> But do not disregard this one fact, beloved: with the Lord, one day is like a thousand years, and a thousand years like one day. The Lord is not slow about his promise, as some regard slowness; but he is patient with you, because he does not want any to perish but all to come to repentance. However, the day of the Lord will come like a thief, and then the heavens will pass away with a loud noise, and the elements will be dissolved with fire, and the earth and deeds done in it will be disclosed.
>
> Since all these things are to be dissolved in this way, what sort of persons ought you to be in leading lives of holiness and godliness, looking for and hastening the coming of the day of God, because of which the heavens will be dissolved by fire and the elements will be melted by the same? But according to his promise, we look for new heavens and a new earth, where righteousness is at home. (2 Pet. 2:4–10; 3:1–13)

The final verse, 2 Peter 3:13, provides us with the key to the larger theological and conceptual context of the above passages and stands as a good summary of much ancient Jewish and early Christian eschatology: righteousness is looking for a home in which to dwell.[56] The point is not about God predetermining some to damnation or his inability or unwillingness to forgive. Rather, the point is that God wants decisively and irreversibly to flood the whole *kosmos* with his own justice and peace, and he will not allow evil and those who perpetuate it to hold the *kosmos* hostage forever.

The above texts, moreover, assume the tradition, going back to Genesis 6 but developed especially in 1 Enoch 1–36, in which "sons of God" or "angels" intermarried with human women, and human beings and the *kosmos* were filled with all manner of ungodliness and injustice as a result.[57] And it was in view of this, so the tradition had it, that God wanted to purge his creation with the waters of the great flood. But what happened to those fallen angels and to the human beings who were lost in the flood? The texts above claim that the former have been kept in Tartarus—itself a tradition growing out of Greek mythology but already adapted into the Jewish tradition well before 1–2 Peter (see 1 En. 20:2; LXX Job 40:20 and 41:24; LXX Prov. 30:16; Sib. Or. 4:186; and Philo, *Moses* 2.433)—whereas the latter have not been kept in Tartarus but more generally in Sheol/Hades until they can be the recipients of the gospel message.[58] And this latter tradition presumes a potentially positive reception, which itself presumes the possibility of postmortem salvation.

But there is, of course, much dispute about these Petrine traditions. Indeed, 1 Peter 3:18–20 has often been referred to as one of the most opaque passages in the New Testament.[59] Nevertheless, I defend my position as follows:

1. I take 1 Peter 3:19–20 and 4:6 together, the latter clarifying the nature of the proclamation of the former: it was a proclamation of the (potentially) saving message of the gospel.
2. While it is certainly true that the language of "spirit" often refers to angels in this period, such language could also refer

to the postmortem state of human beings—that is, to the state of a disembodied spirit (see, e.g., Heb. 12:23; Theodotion's Greek rendering of Dan. 3:86; 1 En. 22:3–13; 103:3–4).

3. Whether "made alive in/by the Spirit" in 1 Peter 3:18 refers to Jesus in the state of "spirit" in-between his death and resurrection or (as seems more likely) to the resurrection of Jesus as effected by the Spirit, the following reference to the proclamation "to the spirits kept under guard" could be taken as I have suggested in items 1 and 2 above.[60]
4. The reference to the spirits' previous "failure to be persuaded" in 3:20 makes more sense in relation to the widespread Jewish tradition of Noah's preaching than it does in relation to the tradition of the Watchers' rebellion and general "sinning" (2 Pet. 2:4).
   a. The characterization of the flood generation as "disobedient" or "unpersuaded," with respect to their rejection of Noah's preaching, appears to have become standardized (Sib. Or. 1:204; Josephus, *Ant.* 1.73–74: Noah had attempted to "persuade" that wicked generation to change their ways, but they refused).[61]
5. The passage appropriates traditions that show virtually no concern over the divine justice of the condemnation of the Watchers (here in chains in Tartarus until the final judgment) *but that do show a concern over the divine justice of the flood*. Genesis 6 nowhere indicates that "God was patient with the *kosmos*" or that "Noah preached repentance to everyone"; nevertheless, such a tradition developed, was widespread (Noah's preaching: Sib. Or. 1:129–98; Josephus, *Ant.* 1.74; Gen. Rab. 30:7; Eccl. Rab. 9:15; Pirqe R. El. 22; b. Sanh. 108; and Apoc. Paul 50; God's patience: m. 'Abot 5:2; Philo, *QG* 2.13), and is attested here. But why would traditions develop in which "God was patient" and "Noah preached repentance"? The most likely answer is theodicy: some Jews were concerned that the way

> in which God destroys the whole *kosmos* in Genesis 6–9 (save Noah, his family, and representatives of the animal world)—apparently indiscriminately and without warning (i.e., all suffer the same fate, irrespective of different kinds and degrees of wickedness)—might be taken to undermine God's justice and goodness. First Peter 3:18–20, in this connection, simply goes a step further. Not only was God patient. Not only did he send Noah to proclaim repentance. But those of this generation in particular were the first recipients of the gospel message following the resurrection.

First Peter 3:18–22 and 4:6, then, give us interesting insight into the way in which at least some early Christians were wrestling with the relationship between God's justice and goodness and eschatological judgment. From this perspective, at least insofar as the flood is viewed as a model of God's judgment, the latter has nothing to do with God's inability or unwillingness to forgive or with the impossibility of some people ever turning to the love of God. Rather, again, it has to do with the fact that one day God will act decisively and irreversibly to purge evil from his good creation.

Revelation

As we turn to Revelation, numerous texts, of course, might be considered. We will focus, however, on the most relevant passages in Revelation 19–22.

> After these things, I heard what sounded like the loud voice of a great crowd in heaven, saying,
>
> > "Hallelujah!
> > Salvation and glory and power belong to our God,
> > for his judgments are true and just;
> > he has judged the great whore,
> > who corrupted the earth with her whoring,
> > and he has avenged the blood of his servants upon her." (19:1–2)

> Then I saw one angel standing in the sun, and he called out in a loud voice and said to all the birds flying in midheaven, "Come, gather for God's great supper, to eat the flesh of kings, the flesh of captains, the flesh of the mighty, the flesh of horses and their riders—the flesh of all, both free and slave, both small and great." And I saw the beast and the kings of the earth and their armies gathered to make war on the rider on the horse and his army. And the beast was captured, and with it, the false prophet who had performed in its presence the signs by which he deceived those who had received the mark of the beast and those who worshiped its image. These two were cast alive into the lake of fire that burns with sulfur. And the rest were killed by the sword of the rider on the horse, the sword that came out from his mouth; and all the birds were gorged with their flesh. (19:17–21)

> Then I saw an angel coming down from heaven, holding in his hand the key to the abyss and a great chain. And he seized the dragon, that ancient serpent, who is the devil and the satan, and bound him for a thousand years, and cast him into the abyss, and locked and sealed it over him, so that he would deceive the nations no more, until the thousand years were fulfilled. But after these things, it is necessary for him to be released for a little while. Then I saw thrones, and the authority to judge was granted to those seated on the thrones. I also saw the souls of those who had been beheaded for their testimony to Jesus and the word of God. They had not worshiped the beast or its image and had not received its mark on their foreheads or their hands. They came to life and ruled with Christ for a thousand years. (The rest of the dead did not come to life until the thousand years were fulfilled.) This is the first resurrection. Blessed and holy is the one who has a share in the first resurrection. Over these the second death has no authority, but they will be priests of God and of Christ, and they will rule with him for a thousand years. But when the thousand years are fulfilled, the satan will be released from his prison and will come out to deceive the nations at the four corners of the earth, Gog and Magog, in order to gather them together for war; they are as numerous as the sands of the sea. And they marched up over the

breadth of the earth and surrounded the camp of the saints and the beloved city. But fire came down from heaven and consumed them. And the devil who had deceived them was cast into the lake of fire and sulfur, where the beast and the false prophet also were, and they will be tormented day and night forever and ever. . . . Then Death and Hades were cast into the lake of fire. This is the second death, the lake of fire; and whoever's name was not found written in the book of life was cast into the lake of fire. (20:1–10, 14–15)

Then I saw a new heaven and a new earth. For the first heaven and the first earth had passed away, and there was no sea anymore. And the holy city, the new Jerusalem, I saw coming down out of heaven from God, prepared like a bride adorned for her husband. And I heard a loud voice from the throne saying,

> "Behold, the dwelling of God is with humans.
> He will dwell with them,
> and they will be his people,
> and he himself will be with them.
> He will wipe every tear from their eyes.
> Death will be no more;
> nor will mourning or crying or pain exist,
> for the first things have passed away."

And the one seated on the throne said, "Behold, I am making all things new!" He also said, "Write this, because these words are trustworthy and true." Then he said to me, "It is done! I am the Alpha and the Omega, the beginning and the end. To the thirsty, I will give as a gift water from the spring of living water. The one who is victorious will inherit these things, and I will be their God, and they will be my children. But as for the cowardly, the faithless, the polluted, the murderers, the sexually immoral, the sorcerers, the idolaters, and all liars, their portion will be in the lake that burns with fire and sulfur, which is the second death." (21:1–8)

Then the angel showed me the river of living water, bright as crystal, flowing from the throne of God and of the Lamb through

> the middle of the city street. On either side of the river is the tree of life with its twelve kinds of fruit, producing its fruit each month; and the leaves of the tree are for the healing of the nations. Nothing cursed will be there anymore. But the throne of God and of the Lamb will be in it, and his servants will worship him; and they will see his face, and his name will be on their foreheads. (22:1–4)

As I said above with respect to 1–2 Thessalonians, the key to the eschatology of Revelation as a whole, and no less to the climactic chapters quoted here, is to appreciate the historical context and the ideal addressees. John, the author of Revelation, had been exiled to the island of Patmos, just southwest of the seven churches in western Asia Minor, to whom he addressed the apocalypse (Rev. 2–3). This is the context of Revelation 1:9: "I, John, your brother who shares with you in Jesus the persecution and the kingdom and the patient endurance, was on the island called Patmos because of the word of God and the testimony of Jesus" (NRSV alt.). Because of their witness to the gospel, John and the churches of Asia Minor had endured persecution, and John himself had been exiled to Patmos.

But what, according to John's Apocalypse, was the nature of this persecution, and whence did it come? Of course, for John, as for many ancient Jews and early Christians (Jesus and Paul included), the primary source of opposition against which the advancing kingdom of God set itself was the dark, suprahuman forces of evil—that is, the satan and its demonic hordes. However, and again, like many ancient Jews and early Christians (Jesus and Paul included), John saw pagan kings, their deities, and their oppressive empires as the primary earthly conduits of the dark forces of evil.

If other indications in Revelation had not made this clear, the gematrial play on the number 666 as the sign of the evil "beast" of Revelation (13:18) puts the point beyond doubt (see also 13:17 and 15:2). In this regard, as many scholars have argued, the number 666 represents a gematrial play—that is, a cryptic use of numbers as stand-ins for letters, words, names, or concepts, something common in ancient languages, where letters had numerical values—on the name Nero Caesar.[62] When the Greek name Nero Caesar (Νέρων Καῖσαρ) is transliterated into Hebrew (נרון קסר), the numerical values of the Hebrew letters (נ = 50, ר = 200, ו = 6, ן = 50, ק = 100, ס = 60, ר = 200) add up to 666. This hypothesis also explains the variant reading in some manuscripts (𝔓115; C; Irmss) of Revelation 13:18, where 616 is read instead of 666. This would represent the numerical value of Nero Caesar's name if the gematria were based on a transliteration from Latin instead of Greek, in which case the final ן (= 50) would be omitted (נרו קסר).[63]

Tidy as this explanation might seem, most scholars, however, date Revelation to the 90s CE, over two decades after Nero committed suicide in 68 CE. How could this emperor, long dead, be the one represented by the demonic beast of Revelation? The answer lies in traditions about Nero's return.[64] As we learn from the Roman historian Tacitus (ca. 56–120 CE; *Annals* 15.38–44), after a great fire had destroyed much of the city of Rome in 64 CE, Nero Caesar scapegoated the Roman Christians. Richard Bauckham comments, "Nero was the first emperor to persecute the church. His persecution, though confined to the city of Rome, was a traumatic experience for the whole church, it seems, not least because Peter and Paul were martyred during it. . . . A Christian apocalyptic tradition which had identified Nero as the Antichrist would be able to maintain this identification after his death by taking up the later expectation of Nero's return."[65]

In this regard, we learn from Tacitus that, because of the varied and contradictory reports of Nero's death, some believed him still to be alive years later: "The reports with regard to his death had been varied, and therefore many people imagined and believed that he was alive" (*Histories* 2.8). And some, of course, made political expediency of the fact that many believed Nero still to be alive. In this connection, we have evidence of at least three insurrectionists claiming to be Nero Caesar from the time of Nero's death in 68 CE to the death of the Emperor Domitian in 96 CE (Tacitus, *Histories* 1.2.1; 2.8–9; Dio Cassius, *Roman History* 63.9.3; 66.19.3; and Suetonius, *Nero* 57.2), at about the time Revelation is usually dated.[66]

In any case, the point of giving so much attention to the historical occasion of Revelation is to get a sense not only of the context in general but of the ideal addressees of the eschatological warnings in particular. John is not generally reflecting on the philosophical, theological, and moral conundrums of personal eschatology. He is, rather, using the graphic language and imagery of Jewish apocalyptic to express the hope that one day God will act decisively and irreversibly to eradicate the demonic forces of evil and their actual or potential earthly conduits. In this latter connection, we should note the two vices that headline the vice list of 21:8: "the *cowardly*, the *faithless*, the polluted, the murderers, the sexually immoral, the sorcerers, the idolaters, and all liars." On this text, Brian Blount and Robert Mounce, respectively, comment:

> The list, which reminds hearers and readers of the one compiled at Rev. 9:21 and anticipates another compiled at 22:15 (cf. 21:27), is specifically designed around the witnessing ethic that has driven John's apocalyptic work. Given John's dramatic call for courageous testimony to the lordship of God and the Lamb despite the drastic consequences that such witnessing will bring, it is understandable that he headlines the list of vices with cowardice [and faithlessness].[67]

> In contrast to the overcomers are all those who have cowered in the face of persecution and joined the company of the reprobate. Leading the retreat are the cowardly, who in the last resort choose personal safety over faithfulness to Christ. . . . The unbelieving

> are not the secular pagan world . . . but believers who have denied their faith under pressure.[68]

In other words, the ideal addressees of the condemnatory eschatological language of Revelation are, first and foremost, the suprahuman, demonic forces of evil themselves and, second, the pagan gods, emperors, and oppressive empire of Rome *and anyone who commits apostasy and thereby joins them*. As with the other texts we have studied, therefore, it would be hermeneutically inappropriate to attempt directly to translate this apocalyptic language into a general doctrine of personal eschatology.

Clearly Universalist Texts?

Now we will deal briefly with a few passages that are sometimes taken as clearly universalist texts.[69]

> Romans 5:18: "Therefore, just as one man's trespass resulted in condemnation for all people, so also one man's act of righteousness resulted in justification and life for all people."
>
> Romans 11:32: "For God consigned all to disobedience so that he might show mercy to all."
>
> 1 Corinthians 15:22: "For just as all die in Adam, so also all will be made alive in Christ."
>
> 1 Timothy 4:10: "For this reason, we labor and struggle, because we have set our hope on the living God, who is the savior of all people, not least those who believe."
>
> Titus 2:11: "For the grace of God has appeared, bringing salvation to all people."
>
> 1 John 2:2: "And he is the atoning sacrifice for our sins, and not for ours only but also for the sins of the whole *kosmos*."

With respect to the Pauline "all" passages, which are sometimes taken to indicate that, among the biblical writers, at least

Paul was an advocate of Christian universalism, I agree with the conclusions of E. P. Sanders:

> The question of universal and cosmic salvation in Paul's thought is potentially very complicated, but I wish to deal with it briefly. One could conclude on the basis of the Adam/Christ passages that all men will be saved. . . . Some have argued that, in principle at least, Paul meant precisely what he wrote, and in support of such a view can be cited the passages on the reconciliation of "the world," where "the world" refers to humanity (Rom. 11.15; II Cor. 5.19). There is, however, a fatal objection to this view: Paul too often mentions those who are perishing or those who will be destroyed on the Day of the Lord (I Cor. 1.18; II Cor. 2.15; 4.3; Phil. 3.19; cf. Rom. 2.12; I Cor. 8.11; 6.9; and the general warning of destruction in I Cor. 10.6–12). . . . What he actually thought is abundantly clear in passage after passage: apart from Christ, everyone will be destroyed.[70]

Of course, some—Douglas Campbell is the most sophisticated example—have employed *Sachkritik* on Paul's letters and thought, arguing that the above passages and others like them, construed in universalist terms, reveal the coherent center of Paul's thought. Any other passages that seem to contradict them, therefore, must be neutralized.[71] It is better to recognize, however, that Paul is both generalizing at the cosmic level (i.e., everything that went wrong with Adam can and will be made right by Christ) and thinking of *categories* of people (i.e., all *kinds* of people: Jews and even gentiles) rather than distinct individuals.

But a potentially interesting question is raised if, with most scholars, we regard the Pastorals as having been written by a Pauline imitator. I am thinking particularly of 1 Timothy 4:10 and Titus 2:11. The former speaks of God as "the savior of all people, not least those who believe," and the latter speaks of the grace of God that brings "salvation to all people." Understandably, both of these texts have sometimes been taken to express universal salvation. But the whole question turns on the force of the noun *sōtēr* ("savior") and its adjectival cognate *sōtērios* ("saving"). Does this "saving" entail salvation from sin and death—that is, eschatological salvation to eternal life—or is something else intended here?

In this regard, I am inclined, with several other scholars, to take *sōtēr* here in a more general sense, a sense that sometimes appears in Israel's Scriptures (e.g., Judg. 3:9, 15) and in contemporary Greco-Roman theology and, perhaps especially, ruler cults, where both divine beings and the Caesars were regularly referred to as *sōtēr*. In 1 Timothy and Titus, this would be a way of talking not about eternal salvation from sin and death but about the one who is the true God and King and Lord of the *kosmos*—rather than the pagan deities and the Caesars who represent them. On the use of "savior/saving/salvation" and "epiphany" language in 1 Timothy 4:10, 2 Timothy 1:10, and Titus 2:11, I agree with Martin Dibelius and Hanz Conzelmann, who write, "This interpretation of Jesus's earthly work is based on the same patterns of thought which the Hellenistic cult of the ruler applied to the rule of the god-king. In fact, the word 'epiphany' . . . appears together with cognates in this context as well; cf. Caesar's title, 'God manifest, descendent of Ares and Aphrodite, common savior of human life.'"[72] Also, as Harry Maier notes, "There is a broad consensus that the formulations of Jesus whose deity has appeared for salvation derive from the Hellenistic and imperial ruler cult."[73]

So we are left with 1 John 2:2: "And he is the atoning sacrifice [*hilasmos*] for our sins, and not for ours only but also for the sins of the whole *kosmos*." With respect to this text, I follow Constantine Campbell, who writes,

> John is quick to add that Christ is the atoning sacrifice not for our sins alone but also "for the sins of the whole world" (2:2). This is a bold declaration of the universal scope of Christ's

> propitiatory act. . . . John Calvin famously understood 2:2b as referring to *the whole church scattered throughout the world* rather than the whole world per se. . . . This has become a common interpretation of 2:2b among those who adhere to a theology of *limited atonement*, which affirms Jesus's sacrificial death paid only for the sins of the elect. This verse challenges that view since it seems, at least on the surface, to directly contradict the position. . . . The most straightforward reading of 2:2b in keeping with Johannine language and theology is to take it at face value: Jesus died for the sins of the whole rebellious world. Nevertheless, John does not endorse any sort of universalism by which all people are saved. Throughout the letter he repeatedly distinguishes between those born of God and those who are not (e.g., 3:7–10).[74]

This is not the place to enter into the debates about how to translate and understand *hilasmos*—whether as "propitiation" (appeasement of God's wrath); "expiation" (purgation, removal, or dismissal of that which separates us from God); or "propitiatory expiation" (purgation, removal, or dismissal of that at which God is properly "angry" and that thus separates us from him).[75] Nor is this the place to insist that, within the context of 1 John 2:1–2, *hilasmos* has more to do with Jesus's *present* work as the resurrected, glorified, and ascended heavenly high priest, ever offering intercession for his people and for the *kosmos*, than it does with Jesus's crucifixion.[76] For our purposes, what principally matters is whether or not this text explicitly affirms Christian universalism. And as Campbell argues (representing the majority position), while there is no good reason to restrict Jesus as *hilasmos* in 1 John 2:2 to "the elect," à la limited atonement,* there is also no good reason to think that John is

* "Limited atonement" is the view that, because none of the fruits of Jesus's death and resurrection can have been inefficacious and thus gratuitous, he must have died and risen only for those who will later be among the eternally blessed. In my view, however, it is better to see the New Testament as variously making the claim that Jesus achieved a universal atonement that is *appropriable* by all people.

here explicitly affirming that, because Jesus is *hilasmos* of the whole world, every distinct individual who has ever lived will enjoy eternal salvation.

Unlimited Atonement

Here, following the above discussion of 1 John 2:2, is as good a place as any to briefly consider the question of the relationship between predestination, election, and atonement. In this connection, I have already argued that the classical doctrine of divine transcendence rules out both hardline notions of determinism and hardline notions of "free will." The reason for this is that both hardline notions presuppose the possibility of competitive agency between God and that which is not God. In this way, they imply that God and that which is not God exist in much the same way and in much the same "space." And to this extent, they undermine classical notions of divine transcendence.

In this regard, the theory of limited atonement has usually been allied to hardline determinism. But we might ask, What about the passages in the New Testament that speak of predestination or election? Might these not be taken to suggest a doctrine of limited atonement? These are the main passages:

> Romans 8:29–30: "For those whom he foreknew, he also predestined. . . . And those whom he predestined, these he also called; and those whom he called, these he also justified; and those whom he justified, these he also glorified."
>
> Ephesians 1:4–5, 11: "God chose us in him before the foundation of the *kosmos* so that we might be holy and blameless before him. In love he predestined us for adoption to himself through Jesus Christ, . . . in whom we also have an inheritance, having been predestined according to the purpose of the one who works all things according to the counsel of his will."

Colossians 3:12: "Put on, therefore, as God's chosen ones, holy and beloved, compassion, kindness, humility, meekness, and patience."

1 Thessalonians 1:4: "We are sure, brothers and sisters beloved of God, of your election."

2 Thessalonians 2:13: "But we ourselves should always be giving thanks to God for you, brothers and sisters beloved of the Lord, because God chose you as firstfruits for salvation through the sanctification of the Spirit and trust in the truth."

Titus 1:1: "Paul, a servant of God and an apostle of Jesus Christ, for the sake of the faithfulness of God's chosen ones and knowledge of the truth that accords with godliness . . . ."

What are we to make of texts like these, and not least of their relationship to hortatory traditions in the same letters that clearly presuppose the actual (not illusory) agency of the exhorted? Essentially, these "Pauline" traditions—Pauline even if Paul did not write all of these texts—affirm *both* divine sovereignty *and* the reality of human agency, wanting neither affirmation to undermine the other. And this comports with what Josephus tells us about the Pharisees (of which Paul was one; see Phil. 3:5): "As for the Pharisees, they say that certain events are the work of Fate, but not all; as to other events, it depends upon ourselves whether they shall take place or not. The sect of Essenes, however, declares that Fate is mistress of all things, and that nothing befalls men unless it be in accordance with her decree. But the Sadducees do away with Fate, holding that there is no such thing and that human actions are not achieved in accordance with her decree, but that all things lie within our own power."[77]

As far as the language of predestination and election goes, this is pastoral theology articulated in retrospect. It is pastoral theology in the sense that it is to be expressed *only* to those who are already in Christ; it is not to be expressed as a general metaphysical principle or systematic position. It is to be articulated only in retrospect. That is, this is not a way of positively affirming a deterministic metaphysic but a way of assuring those already in Christ that God has had this good telos in mind from the beginning. But emphasizing the "chosenness" of those presently in Christ is clearly not designed to emphasize the "unchosenness" of those presently not in Christ. Again, this is pastoral rhetoric.

Even the strong note of predestinarianism in Romans 9–11 ultimately leads toward the statement in 11:32: "For God consigned all to disobedience so that he might show mercy to all." In other words, so Paul is saying—in retrospect concerning the crucifixion, resurrection, and indiscriminatory outpouring of God's Spirit on Jews and gentiles alike—we can see that God has always wanted all people (i.e., Jews *and* gentiles) to be in the position (i.e., in sin) from which alone they could fully see the glories of God's gracious love: "the depth of the riches and the wisdom and the knowledge of God" (Rom. 11:33). Now, of course, Paul would never baldly say that God *wanted* all to sin or that God was directly involved in anyone's sinning. But neither would he say that the telos of the crucifixion, resurrection, and indiscriminatory outpouring of God's Spirit on Jews and gentiles alike is anything other than the telos toward which God's mysterious purposes have always been pointing. In any case, this does not mean that Paul intends to articulate a theology in which the reality of human agency is undermined or in which Jesus died and rose only for some people.

Therefore, no biblical texts directly encourage us to affirm a theory of limited atonement, and 1 John 2:2 stands directly against any such affirmation. At the theological level, a theory of limited atonement would need to presuppose a divine determinism in which the distinct integrity of human agency, and thus divine transcendence, are compromised. But, of course, this does not change the fact that the New Testament, and not least Paul, can speak in a pastoral key and in retrospect about the way in which the salvation and perseverance of various communities have always been in the unstoppable purposes of God.

Conclusion

What I have tried to show, then, is this: whereas the New Testament generally presupposes the possibility of eternal damnation or annihilation, none of the relevant biblical texts directly address the specifics of the eternal destiny of distinct individuals, as is usually supposed. The biblical witness is, rather, somewhat underdetermined in this regard. The following, nevertheless, are the major emphases of biblical and extrabiblical ancient Christian eschatology: (1) God is good and will one day flood the whole *kosmos* with his own good and holy life; (2) it will take a particular kind of constitution (ontology and character) to exist in this new world and to steward it in God's way; and (3) God will not allow evil or those who cling to it to hold his world hostage forever but will one day act decisively and irreversibly to bring evil to its end.

But of course, as I argued in the first chapter, Christians are not only compelled to be faithful to Scripture and to humbly listen to the Tradition's reception of Scripture; they are also called—no less in the case of personal eschatology—to express Christian theology in ways that comport with (metaphysical) Reason. To this we now turn.

3

What May Be Believed?

Weighing the Options

In light of the witness of Scripture and Reason (but with Tradition in mind as well), what may be believed? Indeed, what *should* be believed? When I first began to write this book, I intended to make a case that I no longer intend, precisely, to make—namely, that universal salvation is a necessary entailment of classical Christian metaphysics.[1] In this regard, I simply agreed with John Milbank's assessment on the cover of David Bentley Hart's *That All Shall Be Saved*: Hart's case is "unanswerable."[2] Beyond this, I had long nursed the suspicion that the relevant biblical texts do not directly answer the question of the eternal destiny of distinct individuals, as is usually supposed. So I began developing an argument based on what Scripture seems to allow and what theological Reason seems to dictate. However, in addition to the fact that in an earlier draft I should have taken the witness of the Tradition more seriously, I have actually changed my mind with respect to the witness of Reason.[3] Or to put it more sharply: I am no longer convinced that classical Christian metaphysics, properly understood, necessarily entails universalism. So with both Scripture and Reason in mind, let us finally turn to the major eschatological options open to us:

- *Deterministic damnationism*—the view that human agency is an illusion and thus plays no role in the condemnation of the eternally damned; rather, the damned are predestined for eternal reprobation by the sole agency and will of God. *Evaluation:* Scripture is too underdetermined to support this view; neither does Reason support it. It undermines the doctrine of divine transcendence by placing divine and human agency in zero-sum competition, and it also surrenders any analogical notion of God's goodness.
- *Free-will damnationism*—the view that those eternally damned are condemned not on the basis of divine predetermination but on the basis of their distinct, agential rejection of the saving love of God. *Evaluation:* Scripture is too underdetermined to support this view, but Reason possibly supports it.
- *Deterministic annihilationism*—the view that human agency is an illusion and thus plays no role in the annihilation of the condemned; rather, the condemned are predestined for annihilation by the sole agency and will of God. *Evaluation:* Scripture is too underdetermined to support this view; neither does Reason support it. It undermines the doctrine of divine transcendence by placing divine and human agency in zero-sum competition, and it also surrenders any analogical notion of God's goodness.
- *Free-will annihilationism*—the view that those annihilated are condemned not on the basis of divine predetermination but on the basis of their distinct, agential rejection of the saving love of God. *Evaluation:* Scripture is too underdetermined to support this view, but Reason possibly supports it.
- *Deterministic (dogmatic) universalism*—the view that because God (the good itself) is the efficient and final cause of all creatures, all creatures are metaphysically determined for salvation. *Evaluation:* Scripture is too underdetermined to

support this view; neither does Reason support it. It undermines the doctrine of divine transcendence by placing divine and human agency in zero-sum competition.
- *Free-will universalism*—the view that those saved are delivered not on the basis of divine predetermination but on the basis of their distinct, agential participation in the saving love of God. *Evaluation:* Scripture is too underdetermined to support this view, but Reason possibly supports it.

Deterministic accounts undermine the doctrine of divine transcendence, and ones that postulate either eternal damnation or annihilation also surrender any analogical notion of the goodness of God. Scripture and Reason seem to leave us, then, with three major options: free-will versions of eternal damnation, annihilation, and universal salvation. Now, of course, the notion of "free will" is itself slippery and so will need to be clarified momentarily. But for now, we note a few of the formulations of the most famous modern exponent of the free-will defense of eternal damnation or annihilation, C. S. Lewis:

> There are only two kinds of people in the end: those who say to God, "Thy will be done," and those to whom God says, in the end, "*Thy* will be done." All that are in Hell, choose it. Without that self-choice there could be no Hell. No soul that seriously and constantly desires joy will ever miss it. Those who seek find. To those who knock it is opened.[4]

> I willingly believe that the damned are, in one sense, successful, rebels to the end; that the doors of hell are locked on the *inside*.[5]

But was Lewis a damnationist or an annihilationist? He further comments:

> I notice that Our Lord, while stressing the terror of hell with unsparing severity, usually emphasizes the idea not of duration but of

> *finality*. Consignment to the destroying fire is usually treated as the end of the story—not as the beginning of a new story. That the lost soul is eternally fixed in its diabolical attitude we cannot doubt: but whether this eternal fixity implies endless duration—or duration at all—we cannot say. . . . Heaven is the home of humanity and therefore contains all that is implied in a glorified human life: but hell was not made for men. It is in no sense *parallel* to heaven: it is "the darkness outside," the outer rim where being fades away into nonentity.[6]

However, before we conclude on this basis that Lewis must then be an annihilationist, we should also note the following passage:

> People often talk as if the "annihilation" of a soul were intrinsically possible. In all our experience, however, the destruction of one thing means the emergence of something else. Burn a log, and you have gases, heat and ash. To *have been* a log means now being those three things. If souls can be destroyed, must there not be a state of *having been* a human soul? And is not that, perhaps, the state which is equally well described as torment, destruction, and privation? You will remember that in the parable, the saved go to a place prepared for *them*, while the damned go to a place never made for men at all [Matt. 25:34, 41]. To enter heaven is to become more human than you ever succeeded in being on earth; to enter hell, is to be banished from humanity. What is cast (or casts itself) into hell is not a man: it is "remains." To be a complete man means to have the passions obedient to the will and the will offered to God: to *have been* a man—to be an ex-man or "damned ghost"—would presumably mean to consist of a will utterly centered in its self and passions utterly uncontrolled by the will.[7]

And in this, Lewis is followed in a manner by N. T. Wright:

> The traditional view is that those who spurn God's salvation, who refuse to turn from idolatry and wickedness, are held forever in conscious torment. . . . The traditional picture is clear: such human beings will continue to be, in some sense, human beings, and they will be punished in an endless time. . . .

> A middle way is offered by the so-called conditionalists. They propose "conditional immortality": those who persistently refuse God's love and his way of life in the present world will simply cease to exist. . . . This view is therefore sometimes known as annihilationism; such people will cease to exist. . . . [However,] when human beings give their heartfelt allegiance to and worship that which is not God, they progressively cease to reflect the image of God. . . . My suggestion is that it is possible for human beings so to continue down this road, so to refuse all whisperings of good news, all glimmers of the true light, all promptings to turn and go the other way, all signposts to the love of God, that after death they become at last, by their own effective choice, beings that once were human but now are not, creatures that have ceased to bear the divine image at all. With the death of that body in which they inhabited God's good world, in which the flickering flame of goodness had not been completely snuffed out, they pass simultaneously not only beyond hope but also beyond pity.[8]

But what are the relative merits and demerits of eternal damnationism and annihilationism? Though annihilationism is a modern development (and so not as traditional as damnationism), it has some metaphysical logic going for it. After all, it is God who sustains creation and all creatures in being, and he does so ultimately hoping that all creatures will come to a perfect share in his perfect goodness. But it does not seem metaphysically necessary that God sustains creatures in being—that he cannot, in other words, do otherwise (with the so-called conditionalists). Indeed, as I have just said, God sustains creatures in being precisely with the ultimate goal of these creatures coming to a perfect share in his perfect goodness. In view of this, the creatures so sustained in being must have at least the potential of ultimately sharing in God's goodness (contra Lewis, Wright, and traditional damnationists). And for this to be a potential ultimate reality, the creatures in question would need to have at least some agential capacity for movement toward the good. Without this capacity, it seems they would not be proper objects of God's sustaining love. And of course, for God to sustain creatures in being is an act of free divine love. It would be improper for God to love, and so to sustain, that which has become incapable of any movement toward the good.

Furthermore, it is important to remember that evil neither issues from nor is sustained by God. Evil, rather, is a mysterious privation of the good, neither originated nor sustained by God. And indeed, God would not and could not sustain evil in being, not only because evil is a privation rather than a state of being but because God sustains in being only that which has a capacity for participation in God. Thus, annihilationism at least has this metaphysical logic going for it: if certain creatures simply no longer have a capacity for an ultimate share in God—and if, thus, they have become beings that are no longer proper objects of the divine love (i.e., God's act of sustaining being)—then they simply cease to exist. But then the question arises: Is it possible for a rational creature originally made in God's image and teleologically purposed (in a nondeterministic way) toward the ultimate good *wholly to lose the capacity for movement toward the good*? Perhaps so. But perhaps not.

But what about the theory of eternal damnation? By the same metaphysical logic we have just considered, we would have to say that any creatures sustained in being necessarily retain some capacity for movement toward the good. Thus, perhaps surprisingly, on pain of metaphysical incoherence, those affirming eternal damnationism would also have to affirm the *possibility* of universal salvation. After all, anything sustained in being by God necessarily retains a capacity for movement toward the good.

So far, then, it seems that we can make the following points:

1. God wants to save all people (per Scripture [esp. 1 Tim. 2:4] and Reason).
2. Jesus died and rose for all people (see above on "Unlimited Atonement").

3. God is always working toward the salvation of all people.
4. We must pray for the salvation of all people.
5. Scripture assumes the possibility of eternal damnation or annihilation, though it does not reflect deeply on the matter.
6. The Tradition by and large affirms the possibility and the eventuality of eternal loss.
7. The distinct integrity of human agency necessitates that we affirm at least the possibility of eternal damnation or annihilation.
   a. Eternal damnation or annihilation cannot be thought of in purely retributive terms (on pain of metaphysical incoherence).
8. Everything created and sustained is necessarily sustained by the love of God.
   a. Everything sustained by the love of God has the capacity for movement toward the good and thus the potential for an ultimate share in God's ultimate goodness.
   b. Thus, if we affirm eternal damnation, we must also affirm the possibility of universal salvation.
9. Any so damned or annihilated would be damned or annihilated by their own creaturely rejection of the unchanging love of God.

But what might necessitarian or dogmatic universalists say to the above? They dispute points 7 and 9 and sometimes 5. For example, with respect to point 5, Hans Urs von Balthasar—who was actually not a dogmatic universalist but a so-called hopeful universalist—said the following: "What we have here [in Scripture] are two series of statements that, in the end, . . . we neither can nor may bring into synthesis. . . . And this leads to the second thing. I spoke of leaving open the cleft between the two series of statements. It is not for man, who is *under* judgment, to construct syntheses here, and above all none of such a kind as to subsume one series of statements under the other."[9]

In other words, on this account, some biblical texts stand directly in favor of universalism, whereas others do not. But Balthasar does not commend a strategy of *Sachkritik* in this regard (i.e., pitting one set of texts against another). The most we can do, rather, is to be "hopeful" that the texts that seem to advocate universal salvation will have the last word.[10]

David Bentley Hart, too, asserts that seventeen passages in the New Testament *certainly* affirm Christian universalism, whereas a total of twenty-four *might* affirm this view. As is clear from the previous section, I demur. But what of Hart's much more robust metaphysical case for dogmatic universalism in *That All Shall Be Saved*? It goes like this:

1. God is the transcendent good, to whom no evil characteristics or purposes can be ascribed.
2. Because God, who is the good as such, is the efficient and final cause of human creatures (as creator and sustainer toward a good telos), all such creatures are metaphysically determined to share perfectly in God's perfect goodness.
3. The possibility of thinking and speaking rightly (even though approximately) about God requires the possibility of a meaningful analogy between human language and conceptions, on the one hand, and divine realities, on the other. That is, in this specific connection, human language and conceptions about God as good are either capable of being analogically approximate to the reality of God as good or else our language and conceptions are reduced to equivocal nonsense. Revelation and theology themselves would thus be deemed impossible.
4. But this is not so: revelation and theology are possible precisely because our language and conceptions about God are capable of bearing an analogical relation to the reality. But

this does not, of course, make theological language univocal—as if the totality of the divine reality as such were subject to the human capacity for analogical understanding, such that human analogy could fully grasp the whole of divine reality and articulate it cataphatically. In this sense, Christian knowing is neither equivocal nor univocal, neither irrational nor simply rational, but a knowing that includes, perfects, and fulfills Reason, even as it is capable of going beyond Reason (but not in ways that thereby reject or neutralize Reason).

5. To imagine that God, the ultimate good, might purpose or even allow the eternal damnation or annihilation of creatures made in his image cannot bear any analogical relation to our notions of the good (i.e., it is not supported by Reason).
6. Thus, if God is the good as such, he can neither ultimately purpose nor allow his creatures to experience anything but an ultimate share in the ultimate good.

In this connection, Roberto J. De La Noval has also recently commented: "For the supporters of dogmatic universalism—the view that Christians must affirm that God *will*, and not just *may*, save all—to deny universalism is to render vacuous any talk of God as good: the God who can, but does not, finally rescue all of his children made in his image and likeness is not good in any sense analogically comprehensible to us. To say he is, in spite of his permission of hell for innumerable souls, is to fall off a cliff of equivocation."[11]

I would dispute the above points 2, 5, and 6. Let us take points 5 and 6 first. Here Hart, De La Noval, and other dogmatic universalists are trying to make the creaturely rejection of the love of God—a fact in this present life—submit to analogical reasoning, at least as seen from the perspective of an eschaton in which all are eventually saved. But this is no small metaphysical category mistake. After all, the creaturely commission of sin is one of the sharp edges of the problem of evil more generally—a problem that, by definition, will not and cannot submit to analogical reasoning. And this is because analogical reasoning is legitimate only when it concerns the analogy of *being*—that is, things that originate from and are sustained by God and thus reflect his goodness and purposes. But evil, by definition, neither originated from nor is sustained by God. Rather, it represents a privation and so is precisely not being. Thus, I contend, not even from the perspective of the eschaton will evil be made to make sense à la analogical reasoning. Therefore, it is wrong to imply that here dogmatic universalists succeed where eternal damnationists and annihilationists fail (i.e., that the latter have to surrender any analogical notion of God's goodness). None of us can or should try to explain either the temporary or the perpetual rejection of the love of God—that is, evil as nonbeing—according to the logic of the analogy of being. The rejection of the love of God is no less evil for being temporary.

Keeping points 5 and 6 in mind still, what of point 2? Hart comments:

> For those who worry that this [view of dogmatic universalism] all amounts to a kind of metaphysical determinism of the will, I may not be able to provide perfect comfort. Of course it is a kind of determinism, but only at the transcendental level, and only because rational volition must be determinate to be anything at all. Rational will is by nature the capacity for intentional action, and so must exist as a clear relation between (in Aristotelian terms) the "origin of motion" within it and the "end" that prompts that motion—between, that is, its efficient and final causes. Freedom is a relation to reality, which means liberty from delusion. This divine determinism toward the transcendent Good, then, is precisely what freedom is for a rational creature.[12]

In this regard, dogmatic universalists are setting themselves over against libertarian accounts of free will, the likes of which one finds in, for example, the Church of England's 1995 Doctrine Commission report *The Mystery of Salvation*:

> Over the last two centuries the decline in the churches of the western world of a belief in everlasting punishment has been one of the most notable transformations of Christian belief. There are many reasons for this change, but amongst them has been the moral protest from both within and without the Christian faith against a religion of fear, and the growing sense that the picture of a God who consigned millions to eternal torment was far removed from the revelation of God's love in Christ. *Nevertheless, it is our conviction that the reality of hell (and indeed of heaven) is the ultimate affirmation of the reality of human freedom.*[13]

Hart's rejoinder goes as follows:

> But to me it seems impossible to speak of freedom in any meaningful sense at all unless one begins from the assumption that, for a rational spirit, to see the good and know it truly is to desire it insatiably and to obey it unconditionally, while not to desire it is not to have known it truly, and so never to have been free to choose it. . . .
>
> Freedom is never then the mere "negative liberty" of indeterminate openness to everything; if rational liberty consisted in simple indeterminacy of the will, then no fruitful distinction could be made between personal agency and pure impersonal impulse or pure chance. . . . Thus it is that Augustine could say that the consummation of freedom for a rational creature would be to achieve not the liberty attributed by tradition to Adam and Eve, who were merely "able not to sin" (*posse non peccare*), but rather the truest liberty of all, that of being entirely "unable to sin" (*non posse peccare*). To this state one can attain only when one's nature has been so emancipated from error that nothing can prevent it from reaching and enjoying the only end that can fulfill it: God. Only then is a rational being not a slave to ignorance and delusion. . . .
>
> If then there is such a thing as eternal perdition as the result of an eternal refusal of repentance, it must also be the result of an eternal ignorance, and therefore has nothing really to do with freedom at all. So, no: Not only is an eternal free rejection of God unlikely; it is a logically vacuous idea.[14]

Part of the confusion here is simply semantic. If by "freedom" we are referring to the eschatological state of being *non posse peccare* (unable to sin), then of course it makes no sense to speak of the free-will defense of the possibility of eternal loss. But what we ought to be talking about is the protological state of being *posse non peccare* (able not to sin, but also able to sin) and whether or not it is metaphysically necessary that all human beings ultimately progress from the state of *posse non peccare* to the state of *non posse peccare*—and, if not, how God's goodness is or is not thereby compromised.

Moreover, we should also note that this whole question is complexified in traditions where—as in Augustine and his heirs' doctrine of "original sin," based on their (mis)reading of Romans 5:12—Adam and Eve's progeny are born not in the protological state of *posse non peccare* but, rather, in the state of *non posse non peccare* (unable not to sin). In such a construal, a person's response (or lack thereof) to the love of God depends entirely on whether God chooses to bring them out of the state of *non posse non peccare* into the state of *posse non peccare*. And the problem of theodicy is introduced if and when God does not bring all people into the latter state.

But this is not the way to construe the state of Adam and Eve's progeny. To be sure, Scripture insists that the state of the *kosmos* following Adam and Eve's sin was worse than its state prior to Adam and Eve's sin: it was subsequently ruled by the demonic forces of evil and corrupting toward decay and death (see, e.g., Rom. 5:12–21; 8:18–22; 1 Cor. 15:24–26; 2 Cor. 4:4; Gal. 1:4; Eph. 1:20–21; 6:10–17). But Scripture is also clear that (1) "all lack the glory of God," not simply because Adam and Eve sinned but because "*all* sinned" (Rom. 3:23), and that (2) "death came to all people," not simply because Adam and Eve sinned but "because *all* sinned" (Rom. 5:12).

Thus, in response to the dogmatic universalist position outlined above, I would first appeal to the metaphysical nature of finitude.[15]

To lack an innate and perfect perception of the good or an infallible capacity to choose it is simply to be finite. It is to be not God, not the creator, but a creature. Second, in terms of a defense of God's goodness in the face of the possibility of eternal loss, I would appeal to a "greater good" argument: the perfected, willful intimacy of distinct agents—God and creatures—is a greater good than any wholly deterministic scenario could be. But such intimacy must presuppose the possibility of eternal loss.[16] Dogmatic universalists, of course, reject this and all other greater-good arguments. But this rejection is usually merely assertive.[17]

For dogmatic universalists, to subscribe to this line of reasoning is simply to trade in one free-will defense (the libertarian account in which "indeterminate openness" is freedom par excellence) for another: an account in which one defends God's goodness in the face of the fact that some creatures might be eternally lost on the basis of their immaturity or ignorance in the state of *posse non peccare*. In this case, would God's goodness not be undermined by the fact that he does not part the clouds of everyone's ignorance with the light of the full knowledge of himself, thereby giving everyone an informed perspective from which to choose their beatitude or their doom?

To make this conclusion, though, is to fundamentally misunderstand the nature of the knowledge of God. What keeps people in this kind of ignorance is not simply the lack of certain facts or details about God, Jesus, themselves, and the world. Rather, this kind of knowledge, this kind of move out of protological immaturity and ignorance, is attained only in and as a vulnerable, trusting movement toward God. In other words, this kind of knowledge is not something that subsequently leads to the possibility of faith seeking understanding but simply already *is* faith seeking understanding. Thus, to say that, for God's goodness not thereby to be compromised, God *must* force all into *this* kind of knowledge of himself is both to compromise the nature of this kind of knowledge (which is loving intimacy between two distinct agents) and to bring us back to the problem of competitive agency and wholly deterministic accounts.

But what should we make of De La Noval's charge that the kind of account I'm offering is inescapably Pelagian insofar as it insists on both a distinction between divine and human agency and the necessity (though insufficiency) of a person's willful movement toward God to attain eternal salvation? It seems to me that this is not a problem so long as it is emphasized that the necessary, willful movement of the human agent toward God always occurs in a context within which God is the gracious creator and sustainer of human beings—a creator and sustainer who, having provided for humans' salvation in Christ and by the Spirit, both reaches out in salvation to all people and sustains them in their capacity for movement toward God. In other words, so long as one does not articulate the nature of human agency, or sinful human agency, in such a way so as to undermine the priority of the initiatory and sustaining grace of God *as the context of human agential movement toward or away from God*, then Pelagianism is not a problem. But if any account that is not deterministic in such a way as to render human agency a fiction is thought to be Pelagian, then so be it.

From here we can turn briefly to what Hart regards as one of the most compelling reasons to be a dogmatic universalist: "orthodox Christology."[18] Because Christ "must have lacked nothing intrinsic to whatever it is that makes human beings rational agents," and because Christ could not have "freely rejected the will of the Father, or rejected the divine Good as the proper end of his rational intentionality"—indeed, could not even have "possessed the capacity to do so"—the capacity for movement toward evil cannot be regarded as a sine qua non of human nature as such.[19]

This argument misses the point because the questions are not (1) Is the capacity to sin a sine qua non of freedom or of a perfected human nature? (2) Did Christ have a capacity to sin? and (3) Does a negative answer to question 2 undermine the full integrity of

Christ's human nature? After all, the question is not about the freedom of a perfected human nature at all. Against libertarian accounts of freedom, we should all agree that a capacity to choose the evil rather than the good is *not* a sine qua non of freedom or of human nature as such and, thus, that in the perfected eschatological state, human beings will be *non posse peccare* (unable to sin) and so truly and finally free. Also, we should all agree that human nature will therein have attained its God-ordained telos. Thus, it would make no sense to say that, at least from this perfected, teleological perspective, a capacity to sin is a sine qua non of human nature. But the point is that a capacity to sin *does* seem to be a sine qua non of *the protological state of finite nature*—that is, of human beings who are not the good as such and thus are in an original state of *posse non peccare*. And though it is difficult in this regard to give a completely cataphatic account of how Christ's human will "is in no wise diminished or impaired by being 'operated,' so to speak, by a divine hypostasis whose will is simply God's own willing," we must nevertheless affirm that this is so.[20] But this does not answer the *key* question—namely, Is it metaphysically necessary that finite creatures, originated in a state of *posse non peccare*, all ultimately move to a state of *non posse peccare*? My argument suggests that it is not.

Conclusion

What, then, can we appropriately hope for?

1. Not only can we hope that the God who created and sustains all people cannot but desire the ultimate bliss of all people; we can also be certain of this.
2. We should not hope against God's nature, as this would be to yearn for something other than the good.
   a. Insofar as God's character is revealed in Jesus and then through the Spirit-inspired Scriptures, we should not hope

against the witness of the Scriptures. Still, while the New Testament presupposes the possibility of eternal loss, it is crucial to be sensitive to the rhetorical nature and the ideal addressees of the relevant passages. These passages do not speak as directly to the specifics of the eternal destiny of distinct individuals as is usually supposed.

b. Insofar as God's character is revealed in Jesus and then through the Spirit-inspired Scriptures—and insofar as the Tradition attempts faithfully to interpret those Scriptures—we should stand under the Tradition in humility. But though I agree with the majority of the Tradition that the possibility of eternal loss comports with Scripture and Reason, the Tradition has not always closely followed (or preached) the metaphysics of God as the good.

3. Insofar as God himself, in his conditional will (i.e., contingent on the willful participation of human agents), wants all people to be saved and to come to the fullness of beatitude in him, it is incumbent on all Christians to desire and to act for the salvation of all people. The fact that Scripture and Reason presuppose the possibility of eternal loss should not keep us from hoping, praying, and living for the salvation of all people.

In conclusion, then, God loves all people; Jesus died and rose for all people; the Spirit has been shed abroad throughout the whole *kosmos*; the good news reverberates throughout all of space, time, and matter; the church has been entrusted with the message of the salvation not of some people but of the whole *kosmos*; and one day, God's own holy, loving, divine life will fully embrace the whole *kosmos*. Nevertheless, each creature's participation in beatitude will be contingent on their willful and trusting movement toward God, the movement in which and as which alone saving knowledge of God is found.

Notes

Introduction

1. I refer to Rob Bell's 2012 bestseller: *Love Wins: A Book about Heaven, Hell, and the Fate of Every Person Who Ever Lived* (New York: Harper, 2012).

2. See esp. Augustine, *City of God* 21.

3. On Origen's universalism, see esp. Ilaria L. E. Ramelli, *The Christian Doctrine of "Apokatastasis": A Critical Assessment from the New Testament to Eriugena*, SVC (Leiden: Brill, 2013), 1–222; Ramelli, *A Larger Hope?*, vol. 1, *Universal Salvation from Christian Beginnings to Julian of Norwich* (Eugene, OR: Cascade Books, 2019), 41–63; and Brian E. Daley, *The Hope of the Early Church: A Handbook of Patristic Eschatology* (Cambridge: Cambridge University Press, 1991), 44–64. But Ramelli insists that there are important precursors to Origen's theory.

4. An exception to this is Gregory MacDonald, *The Evangelical Universalist*, 2nd ed. (Eugene, OR: Cascade Books, 2012).

5. For an example of overdetermining the biblical text in this regard, see Denny Burk, "Eternal Conscious Torment," in *Four Views on Hell*, ed. Preston Sprinkle, 2nd ed. (1st ed. 1996; Grand Rapids: Zondervan Academic, 2016), 17–43.

6. See N. T. Wright, *Surprised by Hope: Rethinking Heaven, the Resurrection, and the Mission of the Church* (New York: HarperOne, 2008), 176–77:

> When Jesus was warning his hearers about Gehenna, he was not, as a general rule, telling them that unless they repented in this life they would burn in the next one. . . . His message to his contemporaries was stark and (as we would say today) political. Unless they turned back from their hopeless and rebellious dreams of establishing God's kingdom in their own terms, not least through armed revolt against Rome, then the Roman juggernaut would do what large, greedy, and ruthless empires have always done to smaller countries (not least in the Middle East) whose resources they covet or whose strategic location they

> are anxious to guard. . . . It is therefore only by extension, and with difficulty, that we can extrapolate from the many gospel sayings that articulate this urgent, immediate warning to the deeper question of a warning about what may happen after death itself. . . . Jesus simply didn't say very much about the future life; he was, after all, primarily concerned to announce that God's kingdom was coming "on earth as in heaven."

7. E.g., David Bentley Hart, *That All Shall Be Saved: Heaven, Hell, and Universal Salvation* (New Haven: Yale University Press, 2019), 92–129, is not too concerned with the original historical contexts or ideal addressees of the relevant biblical texts.

8. See, e.g., Anthony C. Thiselton, *Hermeneutics: An Introduction* (Grand Rapids: Eerdmans, 2009), 124–47.

9. On modern Protestantism's failure (esp. issuing from Luther and Barth's influence) to understand and so to appreciate classical Christian metaphysics, see esp. Rowan Williams, *Christ: The Heart of Creation* (New York: Bloomsbury, 2018), 127–41, 169–84; David Bentley Hart, *The Hidden and the Manifest: Essays in Theology and Metaphysics* (Grand Rapids: Eerdmans, 2017), chaps. 1, 5, and 7; and the introduction by John R. Betz in Erich Przywara, *Analogia Entis: Metaphysics; Original Structure and Universal Rhythm*, trans. John R. Betz and David Bentley Hart, RRRCT (orig. 1962; Grand Rapids: Eerdmans, 2014).

10. I adopt the apposite phrase "epistemological Pelagianism" from Thomas Joseph White, *The Incarnate Lord: A Thomistic Study in Christology*, TRS 5 (Washington, DC: Catholic University of America Press, 2017), 194. The tendency to reject the *analogia entis*, and thus natural theology, is particularly associated with Barth and his heirs. On Barth's failure to properly understand Przywara, see esp. Betz's introduction in Przywara, *Analogia Entis*.

11. Mats Wahlberg, "The Problem of Hell: A Thomistic Critique of David Bentley Hart's Necessitarian Universalism," *Modern Theology* 39, no. 1 (2023): 47–67.

12. For the traditional free-will defense of eternal damnation or annihilation, see, e.g., Jonathan L. Kvanvig, *The Problem of Hell* (New York: Oxford University Press, 1993); Jerry L. Walls, *Hell: The Logic of Damnation* (Notre Dame: University of Notre Dame Press, 1992); and William Lane Craig, "'No Other Name': A Middle Knowledge Perspective on the Exclusivity of Salvation through Christ," *Faith and Philosophy* 6, no. 2 (1989): 172–88.

Chapter 1 Preliminaries

1. Formative for my thinking in this area have been Hubert Dreyfus and Charles Taylor, *Retrieving Realism* (Cambridge, MA: Harvard University Press, 2015); and David Bentley Hart, *The Experience of God: Being, Consciousness, Bliss* (New Haven: Yale University Press, 2013).

2. On charismatic experience and miracles, see esp. Craig S. Keener, *Miracles Today: The Supernatural Work of God in the Modern World* (Grand Rapids: Baker Academic, 2021).

3. See, most famously and influentially, Adolf von Harnack, *The History of Dogma*, trans. Neil Buchanan et al., 7 vols. (orig. 1886–89; Eugene, OR: Wipf & Stock, 2020), 1:45–46: "How and by what influence was the living faith transformed into the creed to be believed, the surrender of Christ into a philosophic Christology? There can be no doubt about the answer: these formations are as old in their origin as the detachment of the Gospel from the Jewish Church. . . . The Christian Church and its doctrine were developed within the Roman world and Greek culture in opposition to the Jewish Church."

4. George H. van Kooten refers to this historiographical paradigm as a "Harnackian glass ceiling" in his "The Johannine Christ, the 'Only-Begotten' Athena, and the Platonic Difference between 'Begotten' and 'Made': The Greek Mythological and Philosophical Background to John's Gospel and the Nicene Creed," in *Perspektiven zur Präexistenz im Frühjudentum und frühen Christentum*, ed. Jörg Frey, Friederike Kunath, and Jens Schröter (Tübingen: Mohr Siebeck, 2021), 209–45. See p. 209: "All too often a 'Harnackian' glass ceiling that segregates the New Testament from the early Church is still left in place, while at the same time important early Christian documents such as the Nicene creed are still primarily explained as the primary outcome of inner-Christian debates, without simultaneous contextualization in contemporary Graeco-Roman discourse. I would like to challenge the lingering segregation of biblical studies, patristics, classics, and ancient philosophy, and propose an integral understanding of the development of the notion of Christ's pre-existence from John's Gospel to the Nicene creed."

5. On this, see esp. Chris Kugler, "Judaism/Hellenism in Early Christology: Prepositional Metaphysics and Middle Platonic Intermediary Doctrine," *JSNT* 43, no. 2 (2020): 214–25; Kugler, *Paul and the Image of God* (Lanham, MD: Lexington Books/Fortress Academic, 2020); Gregory Sterling, "Prepositional Metaphysics in Jewish Wisdom Speculation and Early Christian Liturgical Texts," *SPhiloA* 9 (1997): 219–38; Sterling, "'Day One': Platonising Exegetical Traditions of Genesis 1:1–5 in John and Philo of Alexandria," *SPhiloA* 17 (2005): 118–40; Sterling, "Hellenistic Philosophy and the New Testament," in *A Handbook to the Exegesis of the New Testament*, ed. Stanley E. Porter, NTTS 25 (Leiden: Brill, 1997), 313–58; Ronald Cox, *By the Same Word: Creation and Salvation in Hellenistic Judaism and Early Christianity*, BZNW 145 (Berlin: de Gruyter, 2007); George H. van Kooten, *Paul's Anthropology in Context: The Image of God, Assimilation to God, and Tripartite Man in Ancient Judaism, Ancient Philosophy, and Early Christianity*, WUNT 232 (Tübingen: Mohr Siebeck, 2008); van Kooten, "Johannine Christ"; van Kooten, "The 'True Light Which Enlightens Everyone' (John 1:9): John, Genesis, the Platonic Notion of 'the True, Noetic Light,' and the Allegory of the Cave in Plato's *Republic*," in *The Creation of Heaven and Earth: Re-interpretations of Genesis 1 in the Context of Judaism, Ancient Philosophy, Christianity, and Modern Physics*, ed. George H. van Kooten, TBN 8 (Leiden: Brill, 2005), 149–94; Christopher S. Atkins, "Rethinking John 1:1: The Word Was Godward," *NovT* 63 (2021): 44–62; Harold Attridge, "Philo and John: Two Riffs on One Logos," *SPhiloA* 17 (2005): 103–17; and

Thomas H. Tobin, "The Prologue of John in Hellenistic Jewish Speculation," *CBQ* 52 (1990): 252–69.

6. See, e.g., Johannes Zachhuber, *The Rise of Christian Theology and the End of Ancient Metaphysics: Patristic Philosophy from the Cappadocian Fathers to John of Damascus* (Oxford: Oxford University Press, 2020), 1, 3, 5:

> For a long time, early Christian thought has been connected with ancient philosophy mainly in order to explore its sources and to show how the Fathers depended on the insights of pagan thinkers from Plato and Aristotle in the classical period, to Plotinus and Proclus in late antiquity. Scholars who disagreed with this assessment would do so by emphasizing the incompatibility between Christian faith and Greek philosophy whether with a view to censure Christianity for its lack of rationality or to insist on its genuinely religious character. More recently, scholars of both historical theology and ancient philosophy have rightly challenged the stark dichotomy of Patristic thought and ancient philosophy that underlay either of these traditional approaches. Instead, Christian authors have increasingly been treated as part of the late antique intellectual world and as philosophers in their own right. . . . It is the story of their work that will be told in this book. . . . I will show that by the end of the Patristic period philosophical ideas had been generated that were far away from consensus views that prevailed among most pagan philosophers. The term 'ontological revolution,' thus far, is not far-fetched.

7. On the origins and meaning of the *sola scriptura* formula, together with debates about its past and present significance, see esp. the collection of essays in Hans Burger, Arnold Huijgen, and Eric Peels, eds., *Sola Scriptura: Biblical and Theological Perspectives on Scripture, Authority, and Hermeneutics*, SRT 32 (Leiden: Brill, 2017).

8. On the rise of historicist biblicism, one of my favorite treatments remains Michael C. Legaspi, *The Death of Scripture and the Rise of Biblical Studies*, OSHT (Oxford: Oxford University Press, 2010).

9. The best treatment of such Christology in English remains Richard Bauckham, *Jesus and the God of Israel: "God Crucified" and Other Studies on the New Testament's Christology of Divine Identity* (Grand Rapids: Eerdmans, 2009). On the Gospels' divine Christologies, see esp. Richard B. Hays, *Echoes of Scripture in the Gospels* (Waco: Baylor University Press, 2016).

10. On Jesus as an "idealized human" in the Gospels—though unnecessarily playing this off against the Gospels' divine Christologies—see esp. J. R. Daniel Kirk, *A Man Attested by God: The Human Jesus of the Synoptic Gospels* (Grand Rapids: Eerdmans, 2016).

11. For a recent attempt to address exactly this issue, see Steven J. Duby, *Jesus and the God of Classical Theism: Biblical Christology in Light of the Doctrine of God* (Grand Rapids: Baker Academic, 2022).

12. The most famous proponent of open theism in the twenty-first century is likely Gregory A. Boyd. See esp. Boyd, *God of the Possible: A Biblical Introduction to the Open View of God* (Grand Rapids: Baker Books, 2000). The most famous proponent of theological passianism in the twentieth century was Jürgen

Moltmann. See esp. Moltmann, *The Crucified God: The Cross of Christ as the Foundation and Criticism of Christian Theology* (orig. 1973; Minneapolis: Fortress, 1993), chap. 6.

13. Thus, I regard all views that put divine sovereignty or divine foreknowledge in even potential competition with human agency as committing metaphysical category mistakes (so, e.g., determinism, open theism, and various forms of compatibilism [e.g., Molinism]; see, e.g., James K. Beilby and Paul R. Eddy, eds., *Divine Foreknowledge: Four Views* [Downers Grove, IL: InterVarsity, 2001]; and Dennis W. Jowers, ed., *Four Views on Divine Providence* [Grand Rapids: Zondervan, 2011]).

14. As far as I know, no one has made this point about the necessarily noncompetitive relationship between God and that which is not God—a metaphysic articulated particularly in light of Chalcedonian Christology—more clearly than Rowan Williams in *Christ: The Heart of Creation* (New York: Bloomsbury, 2018). See, e.g., pp. xi–xii:

> What I am trying to do in this book is to bring to light one aspect . . . of how the Church's language about Jesus works: how it clarifies other areas of what Christians say and organizes other doctrines around itself. . . . This book argues that a very great deal of what has been said about Jesus across the centuries is shaped by a very particular concern, which has to do with how we think about the relation between God and what God has made. . . . If God is truly the source, the ground and the context of every limited, finite state of affairs . . . , then God cannot be spoken of as one item in a list of the forces active in the world. . . . And this also means that God's action is never in competition with any particular activity inside the universe.

15. On this point, see also Larry W. Hurtado, *One God, One Lord: Early Christian Devotion and Ancient Jewish Monotheism*, 3rd ed. (orig. 1988; London: Bloomsbury T&T Clark, 2015), 22–36, 41–51, 73–95.

16. On misunderstandings of the apophatic element in theology, see, e.g., the recent article by Rowan Williams, "Negative Theology: Some Misunderstandings," *Modern Theology* 40, no. 1 (2024): 243–55.

17. On theodicy in Job, see, e.g., Karl-Johan Illman, "Theodicy in Job," in *Theodicy in the World of the Bible: The Goodness of God and the Problem of Evil*, ed. Antti Laato and Johannes C. de Moor (Leiden: Brill, 2003), 304–33.

18. On Augustine's privation theory of evil, see, e.g., Peter King, "Augustine on Evil," in *Evil: A History*, ed. Andrew P. Chignell, OPC (Oxford: Oxford University Press, 2019), chap. 6.

19. See note 5, above.

20. I am presently drafting an academic monograph on the adaptation of Greek metaphysical traditions in John (esp. 1:1–18), Paul (esp. 1 Cor. 8:6; 15; and 2 Cor. 4–5), and the Letter to the Hebrews (esp. 1–2). The provisional title is *Greek Philosophy and Early Christology: The Invention of Christian Metaphysics*.

21. On the classic Platonic "being" and "becoming" distinction, see esp. Plato, *Tim.* 27d–28a; *Phaed.* 78c–d; *Symp.* 210e–211b; *Theaet.* 152d–153e; *Soph.*

248a–249d; *Resp.* 380c–381d, 382e–383a; and, for a later statement, Plutarch, *Mor.* 391e–394c. On this distinction in John 1, see esp. Troels Engberg-Pedersen, *John and Philosophy: A New Reading of the Fourth Gospel* (Oxford: Oxford University Press, 2017), 50–53.

22. See esp. Kugler, "Judaism/Hellenism in Early Christology"; and Atkins, "Rethinking John 1:1."

23. On the classical doctrine of divine immutability, see, e.g., David Bentley Hart, *The Hidden and the Manifest: Essays in Theology and Metaphysics* (Grand Rapids: Eerdmans, 2017), chaps. 2 and 9.

24. On Middle Platonic metaphysics, see George Boys-Stones, *Platonist Philosophy, 80 BC to AD 250: An Introduction and Collection of Sources in Translation*, CSBPHP (Cambridge: Cambridge University Press, 2018), 81–364. On the slippery category of ancient Gnosticism, see Nicola Denzey Lewis, *Introduction to "Gnosticism": Ancient Voices, Christian Worlds* (Oxford: Oxford University Press, 2013).

25. I take this point to be one of the major burdens of Williams, *Christ*. See also Hart, *The Hidden and the Manifest*, 169–70 (italics original):

> This is, after all, the great "discovery" of the Christian metaphysical tradition: the true nature of transcendence. When, in the fourth century, theology took its final leave of all subordinationist schemes of Trinitarian reflection, it thereby broke irrevocably with all those older metaphysical systems that had attempted to connect this world to its highest principle by populating the interval between them with various intermediate degrees of spiritual reality. . . . And it is precisely *because* God is not situated within any kind of ontic continuum with the creature that we can recognize him as the ontological cause of the creature, who freely gives being to beings. True divine transcendence, it turns out, is a transcendence of even the traditional metaphysical demarcations between the transcendent and the immanent. At the same time, the realization that the creature is not, simply by virtue of its finitude and mutability, alienated from God—at a tragic distance from God that the creature can traverse only to the degree that everything distinctively creaturely within it is negated—was also a realization of the true ontological liberty of created nature. If God himself is the immediate actuality of the creature's emergence from nothingness, and of both the essence and the existence of the creature, then it is precisely through becoming what it is—rather than through overcoming those finite *idiōmata* that distinguish it from God—that the creature truly reflects the goodness and transcendent power of God.

26. I borrow the phrase "negative immanence" from Hart (*The Hidden and the Manifest*, 100), who is, however, commenting on Barth.

27. On the theological hermeneutics of accommodation, see the succinct summary in Alister E. McGrath, *Christian Theology: An Introduction*, 6th ed. (orig. 1993; Oxford: Wiley Blackwell, 2017), 169–71.

28. No one has attempted to make this point more forcefully than N. T. Wright. See, e.g., Wright, *The Challenge of Jesus: Rediscovering Who Jesus Was and Is* (orig. 1999; Downers Grove, IL: InterVarsity, 2015), chap. 5.

29. Though my emphasis on a Christotelic historical-critical hermeneutic clearly has a post-Enlightenment flavor (even if it is grounded in Christology), I am advocating for neither a *sola scriptura* nor even a *prima scriptura* position, in which Scripture and Tradition would be sharply distinguished. While I do think that the doctrine of the hypostatic union commits us to a Christotelic historical-critical hermeneutic (though not to the exclusion of other hermeneutical strategies), I would not, on this christological basis, make a sharp distinction between Scripture and Tradition. Rather, insofar as it represents the earliest reception and articulation of revelation, Scripture is simply the earliest and most authoritative form of Tradition, that tradition in relation to which all later "traditional" developments must be organic.

Chapter 2 Personal Eschatology in the Ancient Jewish and Christian Traditions

1. The manner of my engagement with the secondary literature on extrabiblical and biblical traditions reflects the fact that my exegetical case is deliberately unambitious: I largely take mainstream views on the exegetical evidence unless I indicate otherwise. In this regard, very few historical-critical biblical scholars think the Bible as a whole—or, perhaps, Paul the apostle in particular—explicitly endorses Christian universalism. Thus, there seems to be no good reason to multiply secondary references in the endnotes. What I have aimed for, then, is simply a responsible presentation of the key texts that will command maximal assent among historical-critical scholars, supported by minimal reference to major commentaries.

2. For brief surveys of the extrabiblical and biblical material, as well as of the history of Christian thought (and some engagement with the history of Jewish, Muslim, Buddhist, and Hindu traditions), together with bibliographies, see Jerry L. Walls, ed., *The Oxford Handbook of Eschatology* (Oxford: Oxford University Press, 2007). For the Old Testament, see, e.g., Donald E. Gowan, *Eschatology in the Old Testament* (Philadelphia: Fortress, 1986); Paul D. Hanson, *The Dawn of Apocalyptic: The Historical and Sociological Roots of Jewish Apocalyptic Eschatology* (Philadelphia: Fortress, 1979); and Hans-Peter Müller, *Ursprünge und Strukturen alttestamentlicher Eschatologie*, BZAW 109 (Berlin: Töpelmann, 1969). For Second Temple Judaism, see, e.g., George W. E. Nickelsburg, *Resurrection, Immortality, and Eternal Life in Intertestamental Judaism*, HTS 26 (Cambridge, MA: Harvard University Press, 1972); and Richard Bauckham, *The Fate of the Dead: Studies on Jewish and Christian Apocalypses*, NovTSup 93 (Leiden: Brill, 1998). On Jesus, see, e.g., Dale C. Allison Jr., *Constructing Jesus: Memory, Imagination, and History* (Grand Rapids: Baker Academic, 2010), 31–220. On Paul, see, e.g., Constantine R. Campbell, *Paul and the Hope of Glory: An Exegetical and Theological Study* (Grand Rapids: Zondervan Academic, 2020). And on Revelation, see, e.g., Richard Bauckham, *The Climax of Prophecy: Studies on the Book of Revelation* (London: T&T Clark, 1998).

3. For our purposes, it is not necessary to go into the fraught question of the origins of apocalyptic. In this regard, I'll simply quote John J. Collins's balanced

assessment ("Apocalyptic Eschatology in the Ancient World," in Walls, *Oxford Handbook of Eschatology*, 40–55) at length (here 42–43):

> In view of the lack of consensus among Iranologists, biblical scholars have understandably been reluctant to base arguments on the Persian material. Nonetheless, some apocalyptic motifs, such as the final battle and the judgment of the dead, are found already in the Gathas, and the division of history into millennia and the resurrection of the dead are attested by the Greek writer Theopompus about 300 BCE. Moreover, some of these ideas, such as the periodization of history and the dualism of light and darkness, have an integral place in Zoroastrian cosmology, while they appear as novel elements in Jewish writings of the Hellenistic period. Some influence of Persian ideas on Jewish apocalypticism seems very likely. It would be far too simple, however, to say that the whole phenomenon of apocalypticism was imported to Judea from Persia. It also had roots in Jewish tradition. Other Near Eastern traditions are occasionally proposed as sources of apocalyptic thought. So, for example, Helge Kvanvig has looked for the "roots of apocalyptic" in Babylonian traditions, and W. G. Lambert has argued that "the background of apocalyptic" is to be found in Akkadian *ex eventu* prophecies. These proposals, however, concern the background of particular motifs in apocalyptic literature, not the whole phenomenon. It is generally agreed that apocalyptic writings draw on ancient Near Eastern myths, and various aspects of apocalypticism are paralleled in Greco-Roman tradition. Prophetic material that is somewhat analogous to the Jewish apocalypses can be found in Egyptian tradition in the Hellenistic period. None of these traditions, however, offer such comprehensive analogies as the Persian material, although they may have influenced individual Jewish texts at various points.

4. Bill T. Arnold, "Old Testament Eschatology and the Rise of Apocalypticism," in Walls, *Oxford Handbook of Eschatology*, 24 (italics original), which also cites the following classic studies in this connection: Müller, *Ursprünge und Strukturen alttestamentlicher Eschatologie*, 1–11; Gerhard von Rad, *Old Testament Theology*, 2 vols. (New York: Harper, 1962–65), 2:118; and Sigmund Mowinckel, *He That Cometh* (New York: Abingdon, 1954), 149–54. Of course, this does not mean that, before the rise of the explicit belief in Gehenna as a place of eschatological torment, Jews did not believe in the afterlife, only that our evidence rarely reflects on it. See Richard Bauckham, "Hades, Hell," in *ABD*, 3:14–15:

> The old Hebrew concept of the place of the dead, most often called *Sheol* (*šĕʾôl*) in the Hebrew Bible, corresponded quite closely to the Greek Hades. Both were versions of the common ancient view of the underworld. Like the old Greek Hades, *Sheol* in the Hebrew Bible is the common fate of all the dead, a place of darkness and gloom, where the shades lead an unenviable, fading existence. In the LXX therefore *Sheol* is usually translated as Hades, and the Greek term was naturally and commonly used by Jews writing in Greek. This Jewish usage explains the ten NT occurrences of the word Hades. . . . In most early Jewish literature Hades or *Sheol* remains the place to which all the dead go (2 Macc. 6:23; 1 En. 102:5; 103:7; Sib. Or. 1:1–84; Ps. Phoc.

> 112–13; 2 Bar. 23:4; T. Ab. A 8:9; 19:7) and is very nearly synonymous with death (Wis. 1:12–16; 16:13; Pss. Sol. 16:2; Rev. 6:8; 20:13), as well as actually synonymous with other OT terms for the place of the dead ("the earth," "the dust," "Abaddon" / 1 En. 51:3; 4 Ezra 7:32; Ps. Philo 3:10; 2 Bar. 42:8; 50:2). At the resurrection Hades will return what has been entrusted to it (1 En. 51:3; 4 Ezra 4:42; 7:32; 2 Bar. 42:8; 50:2; Ps. Philo 3:10; 33:3; cf. Rev. 20:13). . . . Hades retains its close association with death and is not confused with the place of eternal torment for the wicked after the day of judgment, which was usually known as *Gehenna*.

5. Translations of ancient texts are my own, unless otherwise noted.

6. See, e.g., P. S. Johnston, "Afterlife," in *DOTP*, 4:

> Finally, Daniel 12:2 speaks unmistakably of personal resurrection at the climax of Daniel's final vision (Dan. 10–12): "Many of those who sleep in the dust of the earth shall awake, some to everlasting life, and some to shame and everlasting contempt." This clearly is individual resurrection of both righteous and wicked. However, it may still be limited. The context focuses on Daniel's people, not all humanity, and the phrase "many of" probably means "many, but not all." . . . In context, they are probably those who die in the final persecution, some rising to be rewarded for their resistance, others to be shamed for their collaboration. So this resurrection envisages the Jewish people, and possibly only one specific generation.

See also Carol A. Newsom, *Daniel: A Commentary*, OTL (Louisville: Westminster John Knox, 2014), 364: "Although the phrase 'everlasting life' (*ḥayyê ʿôlām*) has no exact biblical parallel (but cf. 1QS 4.7), it is similar to God's grant to the king in Ps 21:4 (5) of 'life' (*ḥayyîm*) and 'length of days forever and ever' (*ʾōrek yāmîm ʿôlām wāʿed*). Everlasting life is a characteristic of deity (Dan 4:34 [31]; 12:7; cf. Gen 3:22). The fate of the second group is described through an allusion to the final verse of Isaiah (66:24), which refers to the exposed corpses of those who rebelled against God as subjected to undying worms and unquenchable fire."

7. Ilaria L. E. Ramelli and David Konstan, *Terms for Eternity: Aiônios and Aïdios in Classical and Christian Texts*, PPRT (Piscataway, NJ: Gorgias, 2013), 237.

8. On this widespread and variously expressed Jewish narrative, see esp. N. T. Wright, *Paul and the Faithfulness of God*, 2 vols., Christian Origins and the Question of God 4 (Minneapolis: Fortress, 2013), 2:894–1033, with my critical appropriation in Kugler, *Paul and the Image of God* (Lanham, MD: Lexington Books/Fortress Academic, 2020), 2–7.

9. On different perspectives toward the future of gentiles in Jewish eschatology, see esp. Terence L. Donaldson, *Judaism and the Gentiles: Jewish Patterns of Universalism (to 135 CE)* (Waco: Baylor University Press, 2008).

10. Arnold, "Old Testament Eschatology," 24–25.

11. On the *misericordes* tradition, see Bauckham, *The Fate of the Dead*, 137–38:

> It is very significant that compassion for the damned is thus attributed to ideal, exemplary figures in Jewish and Christian piety. Though the divine reaction

> to their intercession varies in the various texts, there can be no doubt that the apocalyptists approve this compassion. They are allowing the compassion which they and their readers feel for the damned an authoritative mode of expression. It is not a sentiment they consider disallowed by dogma, but one voiced by the greatest saints in direct dialogues with God, in which God at any rate listens. The notion is probably based on extending to the dead the biblical tradition of intercession for living sinners by righteous people such as Abraham and Moses (Gen. 18:22–33; Exod. 32:7–14, 31–34; cf. T. Mos. 11:17; 12:6; 4 Ezra 7:106–11; Ques. Ezra A39–40).

Christian instances of the tradition can be found in, e.g., Apoc. Pet. 3:3–4; and Apoc. Paul 33–43.

12. B. M. Metzger, "The Fourth Book of Ezra," in *OTP*, 1:538, 540.

13. See also Bauckham, *The Fate of the Dead*, 134:

> The apocalyptic idea of the punishment of the wicked in hell owes its origin and popularity to a problem of theodicy. The typical *Sitz im Leben*, at least of the early texts, is persecution, and the damned are concretely the persecutors of God's faithful people and/or the apostates who have escaped persecution by denying their faith. A situation in which God's faithful people suffer and their enemies triumph demands a vindication of God's justice, in the deeply rooted Old Testament sense of justice for the oppressed which has to be at the same time justice against the oppressors. Hell is then fundamentally a triumph for God's righteousness.

14. When I say that the Gospels variously but *compatibly* attest to the same figure, I do not have in mind Tatian-like harmonization. I am simply saying that when we appreciate the genre of the Gospels as ancient semibiographies *and judge them both theologically and historiographically according to this ancient genre*, we will conclude that they more or less give us the same figure, notwithstanding their different narratival, redactional, and theological strategies. See Michael R. Licona, *Why Are There Differences in the Gospels? What We Can Learn from Ancient Biography* (Oxford: Oxford University Press, 2016).

15. On the synoptic problem, I have long been convinced by Mark Goodacre of the Farrer hypothesis: see, e.g., Goodacre, *The Synoptic Problem: A Way through the Maze* (London: Bloomsbury Continuum, 2004); Goodacre, *The Case against Q: Studies in Markan Priority and the Synoptic Problem* (London: Bloomsbury Continuum, 2002); and Goodacre, "Too Good to Be Q: High Verbatim Agreement in the Double Tradition," in *Marcan Priority without Q: Explorations in the Farrer Hypothesis*, ed. John C. Poirier and Jeffrey Peterson, LNTS 455 (London: Bloomsbury T&T Clark, 2015), 82–100.

16. On John's knowledge of Mark, see most recently Eve-Marie Becker, Helen K. Bond, and Catrin H. Williams, eds., *John's Transformation of Mark* (London: T&T Clark, 2020). On John's knowledge of all three Synoptics, see Mark Goodacre, *The Fourth Synoptic Gospel: John's Knowledge of Matthew, Mark, and Luke* (Grand Rapids: Eerdmans, 2025).

17. See esp. Richard A. Burridge, *What Are the Gospels? A Comparison with Graeco-Roman Biography*, 25th anniv. ed. (orig. 1992; Waco: Baylor University Press, 2020).

18. See, e.g., David Bentley Hart, *That All Shall Be Saved: Heaven, Hell, and Universal Salvation* (New Haven: Yale University Press, 2019), 98–101 (citing John 3:17; 4:42; 12:32, 47; and 17:2), who claims that John 12:32 "surely" supports universalism (98). See, e.g., Marianne Meye Thompson, *John: A Commentary*, NTL (Louisville: Westminster John Knox, 2015), 271:

> The point of Jesus' statement that he will draw "all people" to himself is not that he will draw every single person, a point difficult to square with other assertions in John (3:18; 5:29; 8:24), but that his work encompasses all the world's peoples (cf. Rev 5:9; 13:7). The extent of that work to "all" people (cf. 10:16) shows the fullness of God's love poured out for the life of the world. The coming of the 'Greeks' to see Jesus foreshadows the inclusion of those persons who are not the children of God by virtue of their natural descent but by virtue of their birth from God (1:12–13; 3:3–5; 8:39–40).

And see Craig S. Keener, *The Gospel of John: A Commentary*, 2 vols. (Peabody, MA: Hendrickson, 2003), 2:880–81: "His language refers not to the salvation of all individuals (cf. 3:36), but representatives among all peoples (cf. Rev 5:9; 13:7); the context is the Pharisaic complaint that 'the world' was now following him (12:19), and Gentiles were now ready to approach Jesus (12:20)."

19. On "worldview," see, e.g., James W. Sire, *Naming the Elephant: Worldview as a Concept* (Downers Grove, IL: IVP Academic, 2004); David K. Naugle, *Worldview: The History of a Concept* (Grand Rapids: Eerdmans, 2002); Paul A. Marshall, Sander Griffioen, and Richard J. Mouw, eds., *Stained Glass: Worldviews and Social Science* (Lanham, MD: University Press of America, 1989); and the classic studies of Clifford Geertz, *The Interpretation of Cultures* (orig. 1973; New York: Basic Books, 2000); and Peter L. Berger and Thomas Luckmann, *The Social Construction of Reality: A Treatise in the Sociology of Knowledge* (Garden City, NY: Doubleday, 1966).

20. On these basic points, see, e.g., E. P. Sanders, *Judaism: Practice and Belief, 63 BCE–66 CE* (orig. 1992; Minneapolis: Fortress, 2016), 397–494; N. T. Wright, *The New Testament and the People of God*, Christian Origins and the Question of God 1 (Minneapolis: Fortress, 1992), 145–338 (esp. 215–338); Wright, *Paul and the Faithfulness of God*, 1:75–196; and James D. G. Dunn, *The Parting of the Ways: Between Christianity and Judaism and Their Significance for the Character of Christianity*, 2nd ed. (orig. 1996; London: SCM, 2006), 24–58.

21. On this point, see esp. Wright, *The New Testament and the People of God*, 199–301; Wright, *Jesus and the Victory of God*, Christian Origins and the Question of God 2 (Minneapolis: Fortress, 1996), passim; Wright, *Paul and the Faithfulness of God*, 1:139–63 (with the impressive list of scholars who also take this position on pp. 139–40nn262–64); Wright, "Yet the Sun Will Rise Again: Reflections on the Exile and Restoration in Second Temple Judaism, Jesus, Paul, and the Church Today," in *Exile: A Conversation with N. T. Wright*, ed. James M. Scott (Downers Grove, IL: IVP Academic, 2017), 19–82; and James M. Scott, ed.,

Exile: Old Testament, Jewish, and Christian Conceptions (Leiden: Brill, 1997). James C. VanderKam ("Exile in Apocalyptic Jewish Literature," in Scott, *Exile: Old Testament, Jewish, and Christian Conceptions*, 94), comments, "A common portrait of exile in the apocalyptic literature envisages it as a state of affairs that began at some point near the end of the kingdom of Judah and continued to the author's day and even beyond."

For a review of scholarship on this issue, see, e.g., Nicholas G. Piotrowski, "The Concept of Exile in Late Second Temple Judaism: A Review of Recent Scholarship," *CBR* 15, no. 2 (2017): 214–47. See also Jason A. Staples, *Paul and the Resurrection of Israel: Jews, Former Gentiles, Israelites* (Cambridge: Cambridge University Press, 2024), 41–67, which properly insists on the historical and theological significance of the Assyrian deportation of the northern tribes and their hoped-for return in the later Second Temple period.

22. On the appropriation of Exod. 23:20; Mal. 3:1; and Isa. 40:3 in Mark 1:2–3, see esp. Joel Marcus, *The Way of the Lord: Christological Exegesis of the Old Testament in the Gospel of Mark* (orig. 1992; London: T&T Clark, 2004), chap. 2.

23. On John the Baptist and his ministry, see esp. Joel Marcus, *John the Baptist in History and Theology* (Columbia: University of South Carolina Press, 2018), chaps. 3–4.

24. See esp. the whole of the Latin LAE and the discussion in Joel Marcus, "Son of Man as Son of Adam," *RB* 110, nos. 1 and 3 (2003): 38–61, 370–86.

25. On this point, see, e.g., Graham H. Twelftree, *Jesus the Exorcist: A Contribution to the Study of the Historical Jesus* (Peabody, MA: Hendrickson, 1993).

26. Note the following: Joel Marcus, *Mark 1–8: A New Translation with Introduction and Commentary*, AB 27 (New York: Doubleday, 2000), 284 (italics original): "All sins are forgivable except that of blaspheming against the Spirit, i.e., rejecting the ultimate revelation of God's will (in Jesus). But what more precisely *is* for Mark the unpardonable sin, the blasphemy against the Spirit? This question and its existential counterpart, 'Have I committed it?,' have tortured sensitive Christians down through the ages. . . . [But] pastors who counsel such troubled souls that, if they are worried about having blasphemed against the Holy Spirit, they probably have not done so, have good biblical grounds for their position."

R. T. France, *The Gospel of Mark: A Commentary on the Greek Text*, NIGTC (Grand Rapids: Eerdmans, 2002), 177: "This allegation involves a total perversion of the truth and a repudiation of the rule of God. . . . It may safely be asserted that the vast majority of pastoral cases involving those who fear that they have committed or might commit 'the unforgivable sin' have little or nothing to do with what this saying is talking about. It is a warning to those who adopt a position of deliberate rejection and antagonism, not an attempt to frighten those of tender conscience."

William L. Lane, *The Gospel of Mark: The English Text with Introduction, Exposition, and Notes*, NICNT (Grand Rapids: Eerdmans, 1974), 145: "The expulsion of demons was a sign of the intrusion of the Kingdom of God. Yet the scribal accusations against Jesus amount to a denial of the power and greatness of the Spirit of God. . . . In historical context, blasphemy against the Holy Spirit denotes the conscious and deliberate rejection of the saving power and grace of God released through Jesus' word and act."

Morna D. Hooker, *A Commentary on the Gospel according to St. Mark*, BNTC (orig. 1981; London: Continuum, 2001), 117 (bold font original):

> The word **blasphemies** is probably used here, not in the technical sense as defined by the rabbis . . . but, as often, of the denial of the power and greatness of God. Jesus again speaks of forgiveness, this time for all sinners. The one exception to this is the person who **blasphemes** against the Holy Spirit. It is clear from the context, as well as from the editorial note in v.30, that Mark has interpreted this as the deliberate refusal to acknowledge the activity of God's Spirit in Jesus' ministry: it is the attitude which makes a man attribute the work of God to Satan and confuse goodness and evil, truth and falsehood. Such behaviour indicates that an individual **is guilty of an eternal sin**; his attitude of mind is so fixed and obstinate that it forms a permanent obstacle between God and man.

27. For the reading I have just propounded, see France, *Gospel of Mark*, 344:

> How and when it [the kingdom] will be thus visible is not spelled out here, beyond the promise that it will be within the lifetime of some of those present. This time limit is another theme which links the three sayings based on Dn. 7:13–14: the prediction of [Mark] 13:26 is followed by the declaration that this generation will not be over before these things have happened (13:30), and the pronouncement in 14:62 is of what "you," Jesus' judges in the Sanhedrin, will see. These sayings are not predictions of some event in the indefinite and probably distant future. All relate to the contemporary generation. There is nothing here to suggest the *parousia*.

See also Wright, *Jesus and the Victory of God*, chap. 8. For a strong statement of a more traditional position, esp. with respect to the eschatological material in Mark 13, see Paul Sloan, *Mark 13 and the Return of the Shepherd: The Narrative Logic of Zechariah in Mark*, LNTS 604 (London: Bloomsbury T&T Clark, 2019).

28. So also Marcus, *Mark 1–8*, 690, 698: "Elsewhere in the Jewish tradition . . . the OT amputation penalties are often interpreted as symbols rather than literal commands. . . . The rhetoric of Mark 9:43–47 itself suggests that the injunctions to self-amputation are not meant literally. . . . All in all, it seems probable that most of Mark's readers would have interpreted the imperatives in 9:43–47 in a nonliteral manner. . . . It is difficult to know how literally it is meant to be taken in the present passage, since the entire context is hyperbolic."

29. See also, e.g., Marcus, *Mark 1–8*, 690–91:

> This [*Gehenna*], the most common name for the place of eternal punishment in ancient Judaism and early Christianity, comes from the Hebrew *gê hinnōm*, and the Aramaic *gê hinnām*, both of which mean "the Valley of Hinnom," a depression running south-southwest of the Old City of Jerusalem. Here the Israelites, according to the OT, engaged in idolatrous worship of the Canaanite

> god Molech, sacrificing their children to him by fire (2 Kgs. 23:10; Jer. 7:31; 32:35; cf. 2 Kgs. 16:3; 21:6). . . . These associations with death, judgment, and fire contributed to the later Jewish conception of *Gehenna* as a place of eternal postmortem punishment in fire (see, e.g., Sib. Or. 1:100–103; 2:283–312; 4 Ezra 7:36; b. Ros. Has. 16b–17a).

30. See, e.g., the similar comment by Dale C. Allison Jr., *Night Comes: Death, Imagination, and the Last Things* (Grand Rapids: Eerdmans, 2016), 13. He says that Jesus was "a Jewish prophet seeking to exhort, not a scholastic logician."

31. On the whole question of Jesus and Torah, see esp. Paul T. Sloan, *Jesus and the Law of Moses: The Gospels and the Restoration of Israel within First-Century Judaism* (Grand Rapids: Baker Academic, 2025).

32. See W. D. Davies and Dale C. Allison Jr., *Matthew 1–7*, ICC 1 (New York: T&T Clark, 1988), 515:

> Because there is an ascending order of punishments in 5:22—local court, sanhedrin, Gehenna—one expects a corresponding ascent in the severity of the crimes listed. It does not obtain. Anger, rebuking a fellow with *raka*, and insulting another by calling him *more*—one is not more obviously heinous than the others. The difficulty thus created has been solved in several ways—by arguing that *more* is more odious than *raka* and that the uttering of either is worse than anger (cf. Augustine, *De serm. mont.* 1.9.24, and Schweizer, *Matthew*, p. 119); or by claiming that κρίσις, συνέδριον, and γέεννα are functionally similar, each being three different ways of referring to the death penalty (J. Jeremias, *TWNT* 6, p. 975); or by emending or rearranging the text; or by seeing 22a as a general statement which is then illustrated by two concrete examples (so Luz 1, p. 253); or by inferring that the incongruity is intentional and serves as an ironic commentary on or parody of scribal exegesis: as all wrongs against one's neighbour are equally wrong, it is foolish to make casuistic distinctions with regard to degrees of punishment.

In my view, simple prophetic hyperbole sufficiently accounts for the text. See also R. T. France, *The Gospel of Matthew*, NICNT (Grand Rapids: Eerdmans, 2007), 202: "To invoke this awesome concept [i.e., Gehenna] in relation to the use of an everyday abusive epithet is the sort of paradoxical exaggeration by which Jesus' sayings often compel the reader's attention"; Ulrich Luz, *Matthew 1–7*, trans. James E. Crouch, ed. Helmut Koester, Hermeneia (Minneapolis: Fortress, 2007), 236, which speaks of "hyperbole"; and Hans Dieter Betz, *The Sermon on the Mount*, ed. Adela Yarbro Collins, Hermeneia (Minneapolis: Fortress, 1995), 221, which speaks of "parodistic exaggeration."

33. On the differences between this parable and the similar one in Luke 14:15–24, see France, *Gospel of Matthew*, 821:

> The third parable is still spoken to the same audience of chief priests and elders/Pharisees (21:23, 45). There is a partial parallel to this parable in Luke 14:16–24, but the audience there is more general (fellow guests at a dinner). There is the same essential story line of a lavish feast to which those previously invited refuse to come when summoned, to be replaced by a motley collection

of people from the streets, and the conclusion in Luke 14:24 similarly focuses on the exclusion of those previously invited. But the story is very differently told: Luke has no king or wedding, focuses at some length on the reasons for nonattendance to which Matthew alludes only briefly in v. 5, and has two waves of replacement guests brought in (perhaps to represent Jews and Gentiles). He has nothing about the ill-treatment of the (single) messenger, and his host takes no punitive action other than excluding the original invitees from the feast. And Luke's parable stops short when the hall is full; there is no second scene with the expulsion of one of the new invitees. Luke's story is thus essentially simpler than Matthew's, but stylistically more expansive.

34. W. D. Davies and Dale C. Allison Jr. (*Matthew 19–28*, ICC 3 [London: T&T Clark, 1997]) rightly conclude, with most commentators, that "the royal wedding feast is the eschatological banquet" (197), though they note (197n20) that a few church fathers took this as a reference either to baptism (e.g., Cyril of Jerusalem) or to the Eucharist (e.g., Cyril of Alexandria). See also, e.g., Ulrich Luz, *Matthew 21–28*, trans. James E. Crouch, ed. Helmut Koester, Hermeneia (Minneapolis: Fortress, 2005), 50: "In Jewish tradition the image of a banquet is closely connected with the coming new age," citing Isa. 25:6; 1 En. 62:14; 2 En. 42:3–14; and m. 'Abot 3:17–18 (Luz, *Matthew 8–20*, trans. James E. Crouch, ed. Helmut Koester, Hermeneia [Minneapolis: Fortress, 2001], 9n12).

35. When I say "ritual purity," this, of course, is not to be played off against the common notion that occupants (angels and humans) of the heavenly world and of the Jerusalem temple are clothed properly and often in glorious, shining attire. Shining raiment simply indicated that one was in close proximity to the divine presence, for which one required ritual purity. See also Davies and Allison, *Matthew 19–28*, 204: "Because of Rev 19:8 ('for the fine linen is the righteous deeds of the saints'), the wedding garment is, throughout exegetical history, often equated with good works or the doing of righteousness. . . . But, in view of our discussion of v. 13, we incline to equate the wedding garment with the resurrection body or its garment of glory, which were typically imagined to be luminous and angelic." For the interesting hypothesis that behind this text lies a Jewish tradition most clearly expressed in 1 En. 9–11 (esp. 10:4)—in which Azaz'el, one of the evil Watchers (see Gen. 6:1–4), having wreaked havoc on the earth, is bound "hand and foot and cast . . . into the darkness" (1 En. 10:4)—see David C. Sim, "The Man without the Wedding Garment (Matthew 22:11–13)," *HeyJ* 31 (1990): 165–78; and Sim, "Matthew 22.13a and 1 Enoch 10.4a: A Case of Literary Dependence?," *JSNT* 15, no. 47 (1992): 3–19.

36. On the context of this passage in relation to ancient wedding customs, see esp. Luz, *Matthew 21–28*, 228–30. On the clear evocation of Matt. 7:21–23 with the expression "Lord, lord" (25:11), see, e.g., Luz, *Matthew 21–28*, 235: "Later the women arrive after the wedding festival has begun and the door is shut; thus they arrive too late. No one cares any more whether they have gotten oil from the dealers. They call out with the words of 7:21: 'Lord, Lord.' . . . With words similar to those of 7:23 [Jesus] makes a definitive break with the foolish women."

37. See Davies and Allison, *Matthew 19–28*, 418: "Although reminiscent of the earlier parables of separation (13.24–30, 36–43, 47–50), this is not a parable but a 'word-picture of the Last Judgement' [citing T. W. Manson, *The Sayings of Jesus: As Recorded in the Gospels according to St. Matthew and St. Luke* (Grand Rapids: Eerdmans, 1979), 249]. Its special force derives in part from its climactic placement at the end of Jesus' public ministry and at the end of the eschatological discourse."

38. The phrase "members of my family" (or, more literally, "my brothers") is left out of the early textual witness of Codex Vaticanus (4th century), as well as a few other manuscript witnesses, but this is possibly explained as a simple scribal error in terms of *homeoarchon* ("similar beginning"). That is, a scribe might have accidentally skipped over the phrase "my brothers" and gone directly to the next phrase, "the least of these," because both phrases begin in Greek with the same three-letter article (*tōn*).

39. For the identification of "the least of these," Davies and Allison list the following major options: "(i) Everyone in need, whether Christian or not . . . ; (ii) All Christians/disciples . . . ; (iii) Jewish Christians . . . ; (iv) Christian missionaries/leaders . . . ; (v) Christians who are not missionaries or leaders . . ." (*Matthew 19–28*, 428–29). After rightly rejecting (iii), (iv), and (v), they wrongly prefer (i). See Luz, *Matthew 21–28*, 271:

> This interpretation of 25:31–46, which is today the most widespread and generally accepted interpretation and whose central point is the identification of the "lowliest brothers" with all persons who are in need, is not old. It first became important in the early nineteenth century. Contrary to other opinions, it was seldom held in the ancient church, in the Middle Ages, and during the Reformation. Thus on the tree of the history of the interpretation of 25:31–46 it is a young, and in my judgment typically modern, branch. . . . By contrast, the church's interpretation that was the most widely accepted until around 1800 saw in "my lowliest brothers" the members of the Christian community.

For Luz's detailed study of the history of interpretation, see pp. 267–74. On p. 273, he helpfully summarizes a more modern variant of the ancient interpretation, to which I subscribe: "In the eighteenth century a new interpretation appeared that was advocated occasionally in the nineteenth century and that has been advocated with increasing frequency since about 1960. It understands πάντα τὰ ἔθνη to mean not 'all nations' but 'all pagans.' . . . The 'lowliest brothers' are usually all Christians; they are occasionally only the Christian apostles and missionaries. Thus non-Christians are judged on their behavior toward Christians." Luz cites numerous scholars in 273n100.

40. See, e.g., the apposite statement of John T. Carroll, *Luke: A Commentary*, NTL (Louisville: Westminster John Knox, 2012), 335: "Several times Jesus has taken up the matter of appropriate use of possessions (12:13–21, 33–34; 14:33; 16:1–13; cf. 6:20, 24; 14:12–14), so this parable depicting the contrasting fortunes of a rich man and a poor man addresses readers well educated on the topic. The parable enacts the role reversal Jesus has earlier announced with his beatitudes

for the poor and hungry and corresponding woes for the rich and well-nourished (6:20–21, 24–25), which was itself a reprise of the prophetic vision at the heart of the Magnificat (1:51–53)."

41. This is not, of course, a historically objective assessment of all Pharisees. On the Pharisees, see now esp. Joseph Sievers and Amy-Jill Levine, eds., *The Pharisees* (Grand Rapids: Eerdmans, 2021).

42. On "Abraham's bosom" and the tradition-historical background of this passage more generally, see, e.g., Michael Wolter, *The Gospel according to Luke*, vol. 2, *Luke 9:51–24*, trans. Wayne Coppins and Christoph Heilig, BMSEC (Waco: Baylor University Press, 2017), 281–84. See esp. the following from pp. 281–82:

> Jubilees 22:26–23:2 speaks about resting in the "bosom of Abraham" ("And Jacob slept on the bosom of Abraham, his father's father. . . . [Abraham blesses Jacob and dies.] . . . During all this (time) Jacob was lying on his bosom and did not know that Abraham, his grandfather, was dead" [trans. by O. S. Wintermute, *OTP* 2:99]); Testament of Abraham A 20:14 knows it as a designation for the heavenly place of salvation: "The dwellings (σκηναί; see v. 9) of my righteous ones and the dwellings of my holy ones Isaac and Jacob are τῷ κόλπῳ αὐτοῦ (sc. Abraham's); no suffering, grief, or groaning are there, but peace and jubilation and endless life" (for the notion of Abraham's bosom as a place of salvation in rabbinic texts cf. Bill. II: 226). . . . That those who find themselves in the eschatic place of unsalvation can see the salvation of the righteous is part of their punishment and is a common element of early Jewish eschatology (e.g., 1 Enoch 108:15; 4 Ezra 7:83, 85; Luke 13:28–29); the opposite also applies (e.g., 1 Enoch 56:8; 62:12; 108:14; 4 Ezra 7:93).

43. Carroll, *Luke*, 337, notes the irony involved in the rich man's plea for hospitality from Lazarus and Abraham, the former of whom was denied precisely this plea by the rich man in life and the latter of whom was remembered in some Jewish tradition for having been the example of hospitality par excellence: "With striking irony, one who denied hospitality to Lazarus pleads with the figure who epitomizes hospitality toward strangers, Abraham (Gen 18:1–15; a character trait developed, e.g., in Philo, *Abr.* 22–23; T. Ab. 1.1–2 . . .)."

44. On Paul's macrotheological vision, see, e.g., my two articles, "Adam and Christ" and "Creation and New Creation," in *DPL*, 8–11, 212–14.

45. On retrospection in Paul's (christological and pneumatological) thinking, see esp. Douglas A. Campbell, *Pauline Dogmatics: The Triumph of God's Love* (Grand Rapids: Eerdmans, 2020), 1–91 (esp. 72–91). See also Chris Kugler, review of *Pauline Dogmatics: The Triumph of God's Love*, by Douglas A. Campbell, *BBR* 31, no. 1 (2021): 117–19.

46. On all of this, see esp. Kugler, *Paul and the Image of God*, 115–98.

47. Troels Engberg-Pedersen, *Cosmology and Self in the Apostle Paul: The Material Spirit* (Oxford: Oxford University Press, 2010), 8–74, has convinced many that Paul presupposes a Stoic-like material *pneuma* and, accordingly, that the "spiritual body" refers not to a body simply transformed and sustained by (immaterial or underdetermined) *pneuma* but to a body wholly *composed* of material *pneuma*. His case has some wrinkles, but I hope to address those elsewhere.

48. This point about ontology and its relationship to a theology of sacred space is, from the perspective of the ancient Jewish and Christian traditions, crucial. However, it is usually missed in contemporary debates about personal eschatology. In these discussions, a forensic-eschatological framework tends to predominate to the exclusion of other conceptualities; that is, the question of personal eschatology has *only* to do with the divine judge's forgiveness (or otherwise) of the sins of human beings. But in the ancient Jewish and Christian traditions (and in other ancient traditions more generally), what we call morality and ethics are not ultimately divorceable from ontology but in a sense manifest it.

49. Anthony C. Thiselton, *The First Epistle to the Corinthians: A Commentary on the Greek Text*, NIGTC (Grand Rapids: Eerdmans, 2000), 439 (bold font and italics original), gets the point exactly:

> **Inherit God's kingdom** . . . anticipates the theme expressed most explicitly in 15:50. "Flesh and blood cannot inherit the kingdom of God" (15:50) because only transformed humanity can be described as coming fully under God's rule. There is therefore an aspect of "internal grammar" to Paul's pronouncement. *He is not describing the qualifications required for an entrance examination; he is comparing habituated actions, which by definition can find no place in God's reign for the welfare of all, with those qualities in accordance with which Christian believers need to be transformed if they belong authentically to God's new creation in Christ.*

See also, e.g., David E. Garland, *1 Corinthians*, BECNT (Grand Rapids: Baker Academic, 2003), 211: "Paul assumes that since God's kingdom is a kingdom of righteousness, the unrighteous can have no part in it. God's rule brings with it moral conditions that require a radical transformation of values and behavior for believers. Those who practice these sins cut themselves off from that rule and from any hope of a divine inheritance."

50. On the historical occasion of the letter, see esp. the discussion in Douglas A. Campbell, *Framing Paul: An Epistolary Biography* (Grand Rapids: Eerdmans, 2014), 190–253 (esp. 220–53). On p. 221, Campbell writes, "The underlying episode is, as Hugo Grotius . . . suggested some time ago, 'the Gaian crisis,' meaning specifically the plan of Gaius to erect a statue of himself as Jupiter in the temple at Jerusalem. . . . Scholars often resist this suggestion, but invariably for weak reasons." In support, Campbell lists the following commentators: "Best, Dibelius, Frame, Marshall, and Wanamaker" (*Framing Paul*, 221n58). But of course, he also rightly notes, "A principal difficulty seems to be the supposition that 2 Thess was written well after the Gaian crisis" (*Framing Paul*, 221n59).

51. Josephus, *The Jewish War*, vol. 1, *Books 1–2*, trans. H. St. J. Thackeray, LCL 203 (Cambridge, MA: Harvard University Press, 1927), 2.184.

52. Thiselton, *First Epistle to the Corinthians*, 1242–56, considers *thirteen* different interpretations that are attested throughout church history. I here subscribe to the contemporary majority view. See, e.g., Garland, *1 Corinthians*, 716: "The majority of commentators today think that Paul refers to some kind of vicarious baptism for dead persons: 'in the place of the dead.' This view offers the most natural interpretation of the phrase 'on behalf of the dead.'" Garland,

however, like many Protestant exegetes, demurs from this position because "it seems unlikely that Paul would pass over, without comment, a practice that 'smacks of a "magical" view of sacramentalism of the worst kind' (Fee 1987: 764). Such a ritual is not theologically benign, since it completely bypasses the necessity for an individual to express his or her own faith to receive the benefits of Christ's death" (*1 Corinthians*, 717). In other words, it sounds a bit too Catholic.

53. With respect to the ancient church, see, e.g., Luke Timothy Johnson, *Hebrews: A Commentary*, NTL (Louisville: Westminster John Knox, 2006), 163:

> This passage, together with 10:26–29, has challenged readers from the start because of the author's implacable position with regard to repentance. In the early church, as noted in the Introduction (p. 4), the Shepherd of Hermas appeared to reject a position close to that enunciated by Hebrews (see *Mand.* 4.3.1–7; *Vis.* 2.2.4–5; *Sim.* 9.26.5–6), leading Tertullian in turn to reject Hermas (Tertullian, *On Modesty* 20). In third-century North Africa, the Novatians cited Hebrews as a basis for the refusal to readmit those who had caved in under persecution (see Epiphanius, *Panarion* 59.1.1–3.5), whereas Cyprian argued for the readmission of the *Lapsi* (Cyprian of Carthage, *Letter* 51). Ambrose of Milan argued for readmission but no rebaptism (*On Penance* 2.2).

54. William L. Lane, *Hebrews 1–8*, WBC 47A (Nashville: Thomas Nelson, 1991), 142–43, has a good discussion of this point. See esp. p. 143:

> The use of an agricultural illustration of this kind was common in antiquity (e.g., Plato, *Republic* 492A; Isa 5:1–7; 28:23–29; Ezek 19:10–14; cf. Matt 3:10; 7:16). The formulation of v 8 makes a clear allusion to Gen 3:17–18, where the growth of "thorns and thistles" is the consequence of the curse invoked by human disobedience. According to v 8, the sober consequence of apostasy would be the consigning of life to the curse that hangs over a field producing only thorns and thistles, whose "end" (τέλος) is to be set on fire. The significance of the imagery is driven home when subsequently in Hebrews fire is associated with the severity of the eschatological judgment that will consume the adversaries of God (10:27; 12:29; see 6:2; cf. Preisker, *TDNT* 2:331).

See also Johnson, *Hebrews*, 164:

> The author follows this harsh assessment with an agricultural metaphor. The contrast between a plant that matures and yields good fruit and a plant that yields only thorns and thistles has easy and natural application to the moral life (see Isa 5:1–7; Ezek 19:10–14; Mark 4:3–9; Matt 13:1–9, 24–30; Philo, *Who Is the Heir?* 204; *Special Laws* 1.246). The language of "thorns and thistles" is reminiscent of Gen 3:12–18, where God curses the earth because of human sin. The use of "blessing" and "curse," in turn, reminds us of Deuteronomy, where God sets before the people "the blessing and the curse" (30:1). The blessing comes to those who keep covenant by observing God's commandments; theirs will be prosperity in a fruitful land (Deut 30:2–16). The curse falls on those whose "heart turns away . . . and do not hear" (30:17). In the metaphor, to be sure, the fruitful plants are persons who mature in the moral life and do not fall away, while the plants producing thorns and thistles grow

in destructive ways. When plants have repeatedly been cultivated and still fail to yield the expected fruit, they will be cut out and cast away (Luke 13:6–9) or burned (Philo, *Noah the Planter* 17–19). The image of such burning can therefore stand as a metaphor of judgment on worthlessness (*adokimos*); see Matt 3:10–12; 13:30; John 15:6. For *telos*, "end," in the sense of destiny, see Rom 6:21–22 and Phil 3:19; with specific reference to judgment, see 1 Tim 1:16.

55. On the interesting, though ultimately unlikely, suggestion that the name Enoch once stood in an earlier form of this text, see Paul J. Achtemeier, *1 Peter*, Hermeneia (Minneapolis: Fortress, 1996), 253–54. See esp. p. 253: "On the basis of the fact that in the original manuscript of this epistle, the opening letters of v. 19 would have read: ΕΝΩΚΑΙΤΟΙΣΕΝΦΥΛΑΚΗ, with the first four letters (ΕΝΩΚ) looking much like the name Enoch (ΕΝΩΧ), some have conjectured that the name Enoch originally stood in the text (ΕΝΩΧΚΑΙΤΟΙΣΕΝΦΥΛΑΚΗ), with the letter Χ later omitted through haplography with the following Κ."

56. So Richard Bauckham, *Jude, 2 Peter*, WBC 50 (Nashville: Thomas Nelson, 1983), 326: "'Righteousness' is personified, as in Isa 32:16 (LXX: δικαιοσύνη ἐν τῷ Καρμήλῳ κατοικήσει, 'righteousness will dwell in Carmel'). The only feature of the new world which the writer considers relevant is that it will be a world in which God's will will be done. In this he is in the mainstream of Jewish and Christian eschatology. For the righteousness of the new age, cf. Isa 9:7; 11:4–5; *Pss. Sol.* 17:40; *1 Enoch* 5:8–9; 10:16, 20–21; 91:17; *2 Enoch* 65:8; 4 Ezra 7:114; Rom 14:17."

57. On this tradition, see esp. Loren T. Stuckenbruck, *The Myth of Rebellious Angels: Studies in Second Temple Judaism and New Testament Texts* (Grand Rapids: Eerdmans, 2017).

58. See esp. Bauckham, *Jude, 2 Peter*, 249–50:

> The verbs ταρταροῦν and (rather more common) καταταρταροῦν mean "to cast into Tartarus," and were almost always used with reference to the early Greek theogonic myths, in which the ancient giants, the Cyclopes and Titans, were imprisoned in Tartarus, the lowest part of the underworld, by Uranos, Kronos and Zeus. They are not used in the Greek version of 1 Enoch; though τάρταρος ("Tartarus") is used of the place of divine punishment in 1 Enoch 20:2, as elsewhere in Jewish Greek literature (LXX Job 40:20; 41:24; Prov 30:16; Sib. Or. 4:186; Philo, *Mos.* 2.433). But Hellenistic Jews were aware that the Greek myth of the Titans had some similarity to the fall of the Watchers (though Philo, *Gig.* 58, rejects any comparison). Sometimes the Watchers' sons, the giants (the Nephilim), were compared with the Titans (Josephus, *Ant.* 1.73; cf. LXX Ezek 32:27; Sir 16:7) but in Judith 16:6 (and also the Christian passage Sib. Or. 2:231) the Watchers themselves seem to be called τιτᾶνες ("Titans"). Thus in using a term reminiscent of the Greek myth of the Titans the author of 2 Peter follows Hellenistic Jewish practice.

59. See, e.g., Karen H. Jobes, *1 Peter*, BECNT (Grand Rapids: Baker Academic, 2005), 236: "This passage in 1 Peter is the one most debated and written about; from the earliest days of the church, it has been understood in very different ways. Even the usually dogmatic Martin Luther commented as he struggled

with this passage, 'This is a strange text and certainly a more obscure passage than any other passage in the New Testament. I still do not know for sure what the apostle meant' (Pelikan 1967: 113). Even among today's interpreters this passage has the reputation for being perhaps the most difficult in the NT." See also Achtemeier, *1 Peter*, 252: "This verse is one of the shorter, but surely the most problematic, in this letter, if not in the NT canon as a whole, and eludes any agreement on its precise meaning" (citing several others in 252nn146–47).

60. On "made alive in/by the Spirit" as a reference to the resurrection (and thus not to a traditional Holy Saturday *descensus ad inferos*), see, e.g., Achtemeier, *1 Peter*, 248–49. See also Jobes, *1 Peter*, 242, citing several others:

> Therefore, the majority of recent commentators understand the contrasting phrases "put to death in flesh" but "made alive in spirit" to refer either to two spheres of Christ's existence (the earthly sphere versus the eschatological) or to two modes of his personal existence (in human form before his death and in glorified form after his resurrection) (Achtemeier 1996: 249; Brooks 1974: 303; Clowney 1988: 158; Dalton 1965: 14; Davids 1990: 138; J. H. Elliott 2000: 647; France 1977: 268; Goppelt 1993: 253; Hiebert 1982: 149; Hillyer 1992: 114; Horrell 1998: 70–72; Kistemaker 1987: 139–40; Marshall 1991: 121–23; Michaels 1988: 205; Williams 1999: 85).

61. See also, e.g., Bauckham, *Jude, 2 Peter*, 251: "Noah's preaching of repentance may also be implied in 1 Pet 3:20: ἀπειθήσασιν, 'did not obey.'"

62. See esp. Bauckham, *Climax of Prophecy*, 384–85: "The majority of modern scholars find a reference to Nero in Revelation 13:18, where the number of the beast is said to be 666. Since this number is also called 'the number of his name' (13:17; 15:2), John has usually and rightly been supposed to be employing the ancient practice of gematria, whereby any word could be given a numerical value. . . . The practice of gematria is well attested in both Jewish and pagan circles in the ancient world." In *Climax of Prophecy*, 387n10, Bauckham states that this theory was "apparently suggested independently by four German scholars in 1831 (O. F. Fritsche), 1836 (F. Benary) and 1837 (F. Hitzig, E. Reuss)."

63. Bauckham, *Climax of Prophecy*, 388–89, further proposes that the use of θηρίον ("beast") for Nero Caesar in 13:18 has gematrial significance, as the numerical value of θηρίον, transliterated into Hebrew (תריון), would be 666 (ת = 400, ר = 200, י = 10, ו = 6, ן = 50).

64. See Bauckham, *Climax of Prophecy*, 396:

> John is making use of the legend of the return of Nero: Nero, one of the seven emperors of Rome, will return as the final Antichrist, the eighth. But we shall also see later that in his use of this legend in chapter 17, John is especially interested in presenting the return of Nero as a parody of the parousia of Jesus Christ. The beast who 'was and is not and is to come' (17:8, cf. 11) is the demonic parody of God as he 'who was and is and is to come' in the parousia of his Christ (4:8; cf. 11:17; 16:5).

65. Bauckham, *Climax of Prophecy*, 411.

66. See also Bauckham, *Climax of Prophecy*, 413–14:

> The first of the imposters claiming to be Nero appeared only about a year after his death (c. July 69). . . . The second 'false Nero' . . . appeared in 80 A.D. . . . whose real name was Terentius Maximus. . . . At least one more pretender appeared, in the reign of Domitian, c. 88/89 A.D. This one apparently gained the support of the Parthian king Pacorus II and posed a serious threat to the empire. On the most probable dating of Revelation, these events would have been fresh in the memory of John and his first readers.

67. Brian K. Blount, *Revelation: A Commentary*, NTL (Louisville: Westminster John Knox, 2013), 382–83.

68. Robert H. Mounce, *The Book of Revelation*, rev. ed., NICNT (orig. 1977; Grand Rapids: Eerdmans, 1997), 386.

69. David Bentley Hart, *That All Shall Be Saved: Heaven, Hell, and Universal Salvation* (New Haven: Yale University Press, 2019), 92–129, lists seventeen passages in the New Testament that supposedly *certainly* affirm Christian universalism and a total of twenty-four that supposedly *might* affirm Christian universalism.

70. E. P. Sanders, *Paul and Palestinian Judaism: A Comparison of Patterns of Religion* (Philadelphia: Fortress, 1977), 473.

71. See Campbell, *Pauline Dogmatics*, 92–169, 416–42.

72. Martin Dibelius and Hans Conzelmann, *The Pastoral Epistles*, trans. Philip Buttolph and Adela Yarbro, ed. Helmut Koester, Hermeneia (orig. 1955; Philadelphia: Fortress, 1972), 104. See also the discussion of Titus 2:11 on pp. 143–46. And note I. Howard Marshall, *The Pastoral Epistles*, in collaboration with Philip H. Towner, ICC (London: T&T Clark International, 2004), 265: "The passage uses contemporary language from the imperial cult precisely to make the contrast between it and Christian worship."

73. Harry O. Maier, *Picturing Paul in Empire: Imperial Image, Text and Persuasion in Colossians, Ephesians and the Pastoral Epistles* (London: Bloomsbury T&T Clark, 2013), 158.

74. Constantine R. Campbell, *1, 2, and 3 John*, SGBC 19 (Grand Rapids: Zondervan, 2017), 54–55.

75. Whatever the case may be, at the metaphysical level, God's "anger" should always be understood as an accommodative way of talking about the "attitude" of God's holiness toward that which is evil and so destructive of the good.

76. See David M. Moffitt, *Rethinking the Atonement: New Perspectives on Jesus's Death, Resurrection, and Ascension* (Grand Rapids: Baker Academic, 2022), 194.

77. Josephus, *Jewish Antiquities*, vol. 5, *Books 12–13*, trans. Ralph Marcus, LCL 365 (Cambridge, MA: Harvard University Press, 1943), 13.171–73.

Chapter 3 What May Be Believed?

1. For some of the more recent arguments for Christian universalism, see, e.g., David W. Congdon, ed., *Varieties of Christian Universalism: Exploring Four Views* (Grand Rapids: Baker Academic, 2023); Alvin F. Kimel Jr., *Destined for Joy: The Gospel of Universal Salvation* (self-pub., 2022); Bradley Jersak, *Her*

Gates Will Never Be Shut: Hope, Hell, and the New Jerusalem (Eugene, OR: Cascade Books, 2009); and Gregory MacDonald, *The Evangelical Universalist*, 2nd ed. (Eugene, OR: Cascade Books, 2012). For the history of Christian universalism, see together Ilaria L. E. Ramelli, *A Larger Hope?*, vol. 1, *Universal Salvation from Christian Beginnings to Julian of Norwich* (Eugene, OR: Cascade Books, 2019); and Robin A. Parry, *A Larger Hope?*, vol. 2, *Universal Salvation from the Reformation to the Nineteenth Century*, with Ilaria L. E. Ramelli (Eugene, OR: Cascade Books, 2019). See also Michael J. McClymond, *The Devil's Redemption: A New History and Interpretation of Christian Universalism*, 2 vols. (Grand Rapids: Baker Academic, 2018).

2. David Bentley Hart, *That All Shall Be Saved: Heaven, Hell, and Universal Salvation* (New Haven: Yale University Press, 2019). On the notion that universal salvation is metaphysically necessary, see also Roberto J. De La Noval, "Pelagianism *Redivivus*: The Free Will Theodicy for Hell, Divine Transcendence, and the End of Classical Theism," *Modern Theology* 39, no. 2 (2023): 1–21.

3. With respect to the Fifth Ecumenical Council and Origenism, which I have not discussed, see Kimel, *Destined for Joy*, chap. 16.

4. C. S. Lewis, *The Great Divorce* (orig. 1945; New York: HarperCollins, 2009), 75 (italics original). See also, e.g., Jonathan L. Kvanvig, *The Problem of Hell* (New York: Oxford University Press, 1993); Jerry L. Walls, *Hell: The Logic of Damnation* (Notre Dame: University of Notre Dame Press, 1992); and William Lane Craig, "'No Other Name': A Middle Knowledge Perspective on the Exclusivity of Salvation through Christ," *Faith and Philosophy* 6, no. 2 (1989): 172–88.

5. C. S. Lewis, *The Problem of Pain* (orig. 1940; New York: HarperCollins, 1996), 130 (italics original).

6. Lewis, *Problem of Pain*, 129 (italics original).

7. Lewis, *Problem of Pain*, 127–28 (italics original).

8. N. T. Wright, *Surprised by Hope: Rethinking Heaven, the Resurrection, and the Mission of the Church* (New York: HarperOne, 2008), 180–82.

9. Hans Urs von Balthasar, *Dare We Hope "That All Men Be Saved"? With "A Short Discourse on Hell,"* 2nd ed. (orig. 1986; San Francisco: Ignatius, 2014), 22–23 (italics original). On Balthasar, Hart, *That All Shall Be Saved*, 102–3, comments:

> For a 'hopeful universalist' like Hans Urs von Balthasar, Scripture confronts us with something like a dialectical oscillation between two kinds of absolute statements, both indissoluble in themselves and each seemingly irreconcilable with the other. . . . We can at most juxtapose verses of the sort I have just quoted (along with others of the same sort) with other, more ominous verses that speak of a future discrimination between the righteous and the reprobate, and of an eschatological exclusion or destruction of the wicked. Having done this, supposedly, we must then try prayerfully to hold the two seemingly antinomous sides of Scripture's testimony in a sustained 'tension,' without attempting any sort of final resolution or synthesis between them. . . . For myself, I prefer a much older, more expansive, perhaps overly systematic

> approach to the seemingly contrary eschatological expectations unfolded in the New Testament—an approach, that is, like Gregory of Nyssa's or Origen's, according to which the two sides of the New Testament's eschatological language represent not two antithetical possibilities tantalizingly or menacingly dangled before us, posed one against the other as challenges to faith and discernment, but rather two different moments within a seamless narrative, two distinct eschatological horizons, one enclosed within the other. In this way of seeing the matter, one set of images marks the furthest limit of the immanent course of history, and the division therein—right at the threshold between this age and the 'Age to come' ('*olam ha-ba*, in Hebrew)—between those who have surrendered to God's love and those who have not; and the other set refers to that final horizon of all horizons, 'beyond all ages,' where even those who have traveled as far from God as it is possible to go, through every possible self-imposed hell, will at the last find themselves in the home to which they are called from everlasting, their hearts purged of every last residue of hatred and pride.

Hopeful universalism is also the route taken by Dale C. Allison Jr., *Night Comes: Death, Imagination, and the Last Things* (Grand Rapids: Baker Academic, 2016), 118:

> Now I'm quite aware that God's freedom entails, as do countless other facts, epistemological modesty. Perhaps, then, it would be incautious to endorse, without reservation, Isaac and his fellow universalists—Origen, Gregory of Nyssa, Hans Denck, Jane Leade, J. A. Bengel, Thomas Erskine, George MacDonald, Sergius Bulgakov, Jacques Ellul, John Hick, Marilyn McCord Adams. I nonetheless ardently hope that they're right, and I don't understand anyone who feels differently. Even if, as the New Testament more than suggests, God allows some of us to carry our personal hells into the next life, even if there will be weeping and gnashing of teeth, why should that go on forever?

10. While I agree that a few statements in the New Testament clearly and properly express God's desire for all to be saved (esp. 1 Tim. 2:4), I do not agree that any such texts suggest that God will *ensure* the eternal salvation of all people. With respect to the former point—that God wants all people to be saved—one can affirm this and nevertheless give an account of human agency in which the salvation of all people is not certain. In this regard, Balthasar should simply have maintained, as Thomas Joseph White does (in "Von Balthasar and Journet on the Universal Possibility of Salvation and the Twofold Will of God," *Nova et Vetera* 4, no. 3 [2006]: 633–66), the distinction between the absolute and the conditional divine will.

11. De La Noval, "Pelagianism *Redivivus*," 1 (italics original).

12. Hart, *That All Shall Be Saved*, 178–79.

13. The Doctrine Commission of the Church of England, *The Mystery of Salvation: The Story of God's Gift* (London: Church House, 1995), 199 (italics mine). The report goes on immediately to read, in an explicit affirmation of annihilationism, "Hell is not eternal torment, but it is the final and irrevocable

choosing of that which is opposed to God so completely and so absolutely that the only end is total non-being" (199).

14. Hart, *That All Shall Be Saved*, 79–80, 172–73, 178. See also, e.g., Thomas Talbott, *The Inescapable Love of God*, 2nd ed. (orig. 1999; Eugene, OR: Cascade Books, 2014), 185:

> If God is our loving creator, then he wills for us exactly what, at the most fundamental level, we want for ourselves; he wills that we should experience supreme happiness, that our deepest yearnings should be satisfied, and that all of our needs should be met. So if that is true, if God wills the very thing we really want for ourselves, whether we know it or not, . . . what might qualify as a motive for someone making a fully informed decision to reject God? Once one has learned, perhaps through bitter experience, that evil is always destructive, always contrary to one's own interest as well as to the interest of others, an intelligible motive for such rebellion no longer seems even possible. The strongest conceivable motive would seem to exist, moreover, for uniting with God. So if a fully informed person should reject God nonetheless, then that person . . . would seem to display the kind of irrationality that is itself incompatible with free choice.

15. See Mats Wahlberg, "The Problem of Hell: A Thomistic Critique of David Bentley Hart's Necessitarian Universalism," *Modern Theology* 39, no. 1 (2023): 54: "The natural possibility of defection or failure exists by necessity for any being who is not the Good itself."

16. See Wahlberg, "Problem of Hell," 48, whose case, like mine, offers something "that is structurally similar to the free will defense of hell but that does not depend on a libertarian understanding of freedom."

17. See Wahlberg, "Problem of Hell."

18. Hart, *That All Shall Be Saved*, 188.

19. Hart, *That All Shall Be Saved*, 188–89.

20. Hart, *That All Shall Be Saved*, 189.

Author Index

Scripture and Ancient Writings Index